AF413836

The Accidental Picasso Thief

The Accidental Picasso Thief

The True Story of a Reverse Heist, Outrunning the FBI, and Fleeing the Boston Mob

by Whit Rummel

with Noah Charney

BLOOMSBURY ACADEMIC

NEW YORK · LONDON · OXFORD · NEW DELHI · SYDNEY

BLOOMSBURY ACADEMIC
Bloomsbury Publishing Inc, 1359 Broadway, 12th Floor, New York, NY 10018, USA
Bloomsbury Publishing Plc, 50 Bedford Square, London, WC1B 3DP, UK
Bloomsbury Publishing Ireland, 29 Earlsfort Terrace, Dublin 2, D02 AY28, Ireland

BLOOMSBURY, BLOOMSBURY ACADEMIC and the Diana logo are trademarks of Bloomsbury
Publishing Plc

First published in the United States of America 2026

Copyright © Bloomsbury Publishing, 2026

Cover image courtesy of Whit C. Rummel
Cover design by Kathi Ha

Bloomsbury Publishing Inc does not have any control over, or responsibility for, any third-party websites
referred to or in this book. All internet addresses given in this book were correct at the time of going
to press. The author and publisher regret any inconvenience caused if addresses have changed or sites
have ceased to exist, but can accept no responsibility for any such changes.

Library of Congress Cataloging-in-Publication Data
Names: Rummel, Whit, 1947- author | Charney, Noah author
Title: The accidental Picasso thief : the true story of a reverse heist, outrunning the FBI,
and fleeing the Boston mob / by Whit Rummel with Noah Charney.
Description: First edition. | New York : Bloomsbury Academic, 2025. |
Includes bibliographical references and index.
Identifiers: LCCN 2025019167 | ISBN 9798765188262 hardcover |
ISBN 9798765188279 epub | ISBN 9798765188286 pdf
Subjects: LCSH: Picasso, Pablo, 1881-1973 Portrait of a woman and a musketeer |
Art thefts—Massachusetts—Boston
Classification: LCC ND553.P5 A7825 2025 | DDC
364.16/287594—dc23/eng/20250625

LC record available at https://lccn.loc.gov/2025019167

ISBN: HB: 979-8-7651-8826-2
ePDF: 979-8-7651-8828-6
eBook: 979-8-7651-8827-9

Typeset by Deanta Global Publishing Services, Chennai, India
Printed and bound in the United States of America

For product safety related questions contact productsafety@bloomsbury.com.

To find out more about our authors and books visit www.bloomsbury.com and sign up
for our newsletters.

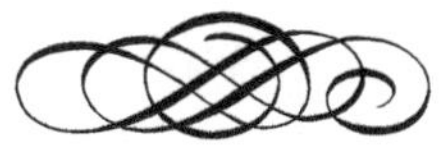

Contents

Part III The Mystery 101

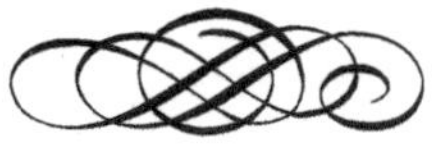

Acknowledgments

First of all, thanks to Charles Harmon, Editorial Director at Bloomsbury, without whom none of this would have been possible. Great gratitude to Noah Charney, who got this whole idea off the ground to begin with. Credit also goes to Daniel Wallace, for his ceaseless and enduring encouragement. Infinite gratitude to my brother, Bill, because he started the whole thing in the first place. I'd also like to thank his widow, Sam, whose memories of him over their longtime marriage were invaluable. Loads of kudos to my son Whit, who's been a key part of the Picasso search party ever since he was a small child. Finally, endless credit to my wonderful wife, Christen, mentor and muse for forty years.

—Whit Rummel

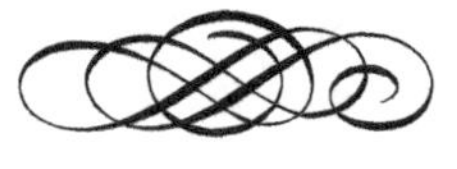

Introduction

This book is the true story of one of the oddest art crimes in American history. But the stealing part was easy. In fact, it happened by accident. The real trick, the actual danger, was in undoing the theft. It required a reverse heist to get the painting back to where it belonged without those involved in having stolen it getting arrested, or maybe even "offed."

We've elected to tell that story in an unusual way. You'll see that there are two authors, Whit Rummel "with" Noah Charney. Most of the story involves Whit telling the tale to Noah, and Noah writing it up. It's a first-person narrative, told in Whit's voice, because Whit was there. He was one of the three protagonists, along with his brother, Bill, and his father, Whit Senior. In order to keep Whit's unique and engaging voice, the story is written as if he were telling it to you, perhaps while sitting on the deck of his North Carolina home, with the wind in the trees and the song of birds peppering the soundtrack. Even this Introduction is being written by Noah in Whit's voice.

It's a great advantage to recount a piece of American history from the account of someone who was actually there. We've embraced this and chosen to tell the story in a novelistic style, including dialogue. Much of that dialogue is real, as close to word-for-word as Whit can remember, or can remember being told how it went when he wasn't there in person. Some parts of it are imagined based on extensive, intimate knowledge of the speakers. This is no new technique—plenty of non-fiction books use a novelistic, cinematic approach and include dialogue that is probably pretty accurate to real life but can't be confirmed in archival sources. Our approach tips our hat to such authors and allows us to take full advantage of telling a story straight from the proverbial horse's mouth. Noah's goal was to cleave as tightly as possible to the words of said horse (that'd be Whit), while shaping the narrative into a book and supplementing Whit's memories with newspaper clippings and other archival material. And there's plenty of it, because Whit's father was often in the news long before the Picasso event took place. But when it did, it made international headlines.

Whit and Noah found each other when *The New York Times* ran a feature on the theft entitled "Hey Dad, Can You Help Me Return the Picasso I Stole?" written by Dan Barry and published on June 15, 2023.[1] Whit reached out to Noah, who is renowned as an expert on the history of art crime, to see if there was interest in turning the story into a book.

The main source for that article, and this book, was Whit himself. For that reason, this book is lightly cited, as it would get old quickly to have hundreds of citations of facts listed as "interview with the author." Instead, we've cited only quotes taken from newspapers and facts from sources other than Whit Rummel Jr.

We've divided the book into three sections. Part I kicks off with a quick snapshot of the reverse heist but then focuses on introducing the three protagonists, their characters, and the milieu in which they grew up—as with any good caper, you first get to know the team, ending with one fateful day in February 1969 when three life-changing events happened to the three protagonists and, as fate would have it, all taking place on the very same day.

Part II takes place in the winter of 1969 in Boston and deals first with the theft, then the eventual return of the stolen Picasso painting, *La Mademoiselle et Le Mousquetaire*.

Part III follows the story through the decades that followed to today, as Whit made it his mission to track down the Picasso, which had mysteriously vanished soon after its return in 1969. It also includes a set-piece of when the first American buyer, Irving Luntz, acquired it from Picasso's famous gallerist, Henry-David Kahnweiler—the details were told to me by Luntz himself.

We hope you enjoy the read as much as we enjoyed writing it. And—Authors' Message—if you ever end up with a stolen painting, however it might have come into your hands, do the right thing and return it. For your own good, if no one else's.

—Whit Rummel and Noah Charney

Part I

The Setup

1

Boston

April 1, 1969

"Slow down, damn it."

The 1962 black Chevy Impala Super Sport made its way past Boston's Museum of Fine Arts. It's keeping pace with traffic, but the young driver follows the older passenger's command, more out of habit than necessity.

Everything's going according to plan. So far.

The two men in the Chevy look like caricatures of no-goodniks, but then that concept of what a "bad guy" looks like is surely based on the real thing, isn't it? The older man, in his late fifties, wears a dark trench coat with the collar turned up and a black fedora, along with a pair of wraparound shades. He's also sporting an off-balance handlebar mustache that looks fake from twenty paces. The younger man, in his early twenties, wears a navy peacoat, his collar popped too, and a watch cap pulled down low. A pair of reflector aviators hide his eyes. He maneuvers the car with white knuckles, but you can't see them through his black leather gloves.

It happens to be April Fool's Day—no coincidence—and the year is 1969.

Traffic is slow for 2 p.m., perhaps because the cold, light rain has driven pedestrians into cabs. The Chevy makes another pass in front of the museum.

The mighty bronze statue out front, *Appeal to the Great Spirit* by Cyrus Dallin, is of a Native American on horseback, arms outstretched, now aged to the color of mint. The MFA itself is modeled on an ancient Greek temple, all Ionic columns and honey-colored stone.

The young driver turns on the radio to cut the tension. On comes "The End" by the Doors. The older man looks over in disapproval and pushes a button to change the station. A news announcer's voice comes on:

The chances that an international ring of art thieves is specializing in stealing the works of Pablo Picasso grew stronger Saturday as detectives noted similarities between two daring art thefts in Boston. One was the holdup of Back Bay art dealer Alan Fink in his Newbury Street gallery in which 40 etchings of the famed Spanish master, valued at more than $25,000, were taken by bandits who seemed to know exactly what they were looking for. The other is a . . .

The older man kills the radio as the two men look at each other.

"Here. Up on the left," he says. "Turn in."

The driver passes the MFA's Huntington Street entrance to a side road where he makes a quick turn into a parking lot. The Chevy glides down a slight decline and approaches the museum loading dock. There's nobody in sight. The driver stops in front of one of the bays and slams the car into park.

The older man pops the door handle and starts to get out.

Suddenly, three MFA employees emerge. They're chatting and joking loudly, pulling out cigarettes for their smoke break.

"Damn it," the older man says. "Get out of here. Now."

The Chevy reverses. The smokers don't seem to notice, at least not until the young driver hits the gas a little too hard and squeals the tires as the car pulls away.

Time for Plan B.

The Chevy turns onto Louis Prang Street, then onto Fenway. On their left is the Isabella Stewart Gardner Museum, a misplaced Venetian Gothic palace in the heart of Boston (which won't be robbed for another twenty-one years). The Chevy continues to weave its way downtown, ending up on Boylston Street near the Commons.

"Pull up over there," the older man says. The driver stops opposite a swanky hotel. An oversized American flag sways in the chill breeze above the entrance. The words "The Ritz-Carlton" are clearly visible on a large overhead awning.

Traffic whizzes past, honking angrily at the Chevy's abrupt stop.

The old man opens the door and then leans back in to address the driver.

"If I'm not back in three minutes, get the hell out of here."

"Yes, Dad," the younger man replies.

2

Waterville, Maine

Whitcomb Mercer Rummel Sr. always had a sharp eye for investment and opportunity. With his longtime friend and partner Dr. Irving I. Goodof, he loved to invest in potential development property. His success was such that an October 1968 article in Waterville's *Morning Sentinel* outlined his approach, based on an interview with him.

This city . . . has seen quite an example of what can be done in this age of development off the interstates—if you come in at the right time and if you develop property. Some year ago, Dr. Irving I. Goodof asked Whitcomb M. Rummel, a close friend and owner of Rummel's Ice Cream on Silver St., to do some real estate investing with him. As Rummel tells it, that's all it was meant to be. The investment was to be in land on Kennedy Memorial Drive next to Interstate 95 at the Oakland-Waterville exit. Pieces of land were purchased by the two and were held. One has been sold so far, Rummel, says. That cost $14,000 and was sold for more than $30,000, he reveals.

The pieces purchased were in a line going toward the interstate. The final piece purchased was right next to the exit and had a place called "Reggie's Steak House" on it. The place was bankrupt and closed down, Rummel explains. "We had absolutely no intention of having a restaurant there when we bought the land," he says.

Some thought changed the minds of the two new owners. They didn't want to see the building go to waste. They brought in a chef from Boston, let him run the place. He lost $8000 the first year. A change in décor was made. Another chef took the spot over for the two. Again, there were losses.

"We finally got the idea," Rummel says. ". . . I took over active operation of the place about three years ago." A name that was different was sought. The two came up with "The Silent Woman." This was a name used on restaurants and taverns all over Europe. It had also been used in this country, as early as colonial times. The Silent Woman is headless. She's featured on the restaurant's menus with a description of her background and quotes about her.

Rummel went to England, picked up some Vanity Fair prints made by Spy. These went up on the walls. The waitresses were fitted out with a garb somewhat like that of Thackeray days in England. The menu came out with Dickens characters on it drawn by artist Paul Plummer Jr. Up over a door went a painting of a hangmen titled simply "Our Founder."

That differentness wasn't carried to an extreme, however. And the chief attraction of the spot now has to be its food and the prices of that food. This reporter knows from experience. The food is excellent and the prices are low. Word has got around about the Silent Woman. Rummel showed me his sales for the year. He keeps a week-by-week check of the percentage rise. Some weeks have shown a 30 percent increase, some a 40 percent rise, the highest was more than 80 percent.

"Reggie's Steak House" seated about 80. So does the "Silent Woman." But in a couple of months, the restaurant will have places for about 350. A $100,000 renovation and expansion is doing that job.[1]

It was all going so brilliantly for Whit Rummel Sr. At least until late February of 1969. That's when he got the phone call.

But before we catch up with that ominous phone ring, we need to set the scene because it's not yet 1969. And to understand Bill, and the accidental theft that changed his life and bookmarked itself in American history, you need to meet Bill's father.

Bill wasn't the only member of the Rummel family to attain the rank of SK5 in military service. His father Whit also hit that point when he was discharged from the Navy Seabees at the end of World War II. The Seabees were the United States Naval Construction Battalions, effectively the Navy's engineering corps. They were involved in construction, everything from bridges to bunkers, bases to roads to airfields. Their logo is a six-armed bee wearing a white navy hat, carrying a machine gun, a wrench, and a hammer. Their slogan: "Can do!" It was a good slogan for Whit Rummel Sr.

He had served in North Africa and returned from the war keen to start his "own thing" as he liked to call it, whatever "it" might be. He'd been one of Clarence Birdseye's first salesmen, selling frozen foods before frozen foods was a thing. He was good at it too, a natural, chatty, and amiable, but that wasn't *his* thing. He was sure he wanted to run his own business, be his own boss, and dole out the guff rather than take it from anyone else.

One weekend he and his wife, Ann, and their three-year-old son, Merrill (Bill to everyone who knew him), drove up to Waterville, Maine, to visit his mother-in-law, Florence.

In the late 1940s, Waterville, Maine, was a small but bustling mill town, perched on the banks of the Kennebec River. The paper mills and textile factories that powered its economy filled the air with the constant hum of industry, and a faint scent of wood pulp and steam seemed to hang over the town. Cobblestone streets bustled with the energy of workers heading to their shifts, while the storefronts lining Main Street echoed the postwar optimism. Bright, neon signs advertised diners, drugstores, and five-and-dime shops that brimmed with new consumer goods—the American Dream packaged in colorful displays.

Waterville's downtown area was a place where neighbors greeted one another by name, exchanging news and gossip on the sidewalks or over a cup of coffee at a local café. The architecture, a mix of brick storefronts and modest wooden houses, reflected the town's working-class roots, though some stately Victorian homes still hinted at its more prosperous past. Colby College, perched on a hill overlooking the town, brought an air of intellectualism to the community, its students, and faculty providing a contrast to the mill workers in their blue-collar attire. They didn't always get along, but the townsfolk were proud of the college atop a nearby hill.

The town's social life was anchored by church gatherings, local baseball games, and the occasional dance at the town hall, where big band music would draw young couples to the floor. The postwar era had brought both hope and a sense of change—veterans returned home, families grew, and the future seemed wide open. Yet Waterville retained its Maine stoicism, a quiet resilience in the face of both prosperity and the challenges of an industrial town slowly beginning to evolve. It was a waspy, gee-whiz kind of place. The sort you'd have seen made into film sets in countless black-and-white TV shows and movies of the 1950s, with the five-and-dime and the soda fountain and kids playing stickball in backyards and paperboys bicycling through early mornings.

If Waterville had royalty, Whit's wife Ann was it. She was a Thayer, and there were plenty of places, buildings, and roads named Thayer in town. Her father, Eugene Lorenzo Thayer, had been mayor and something of a town hero, as he led Waterville through the Great Depression.

He was first elected in 1933 and reelected in 1934 with a record-breaking majority. One of his most significant contributions as mayor was overseeing the town's relief efforts during the Depression and helping restore Waterville's financial stability after local banks had closed. His leadership successfully reestablished the town's credit—no small task—providing much-needed stability during an economically turbulent period.

Thayer was also involved in administering federal aid programs, such as the Civil Works Administration and the Emergency Relief Administration, helping those in need within the community. He became the only mayor of Waterville to pass away while in office, dying of a brain hemorrhage in September 1934. In recognition of his contributions, a bridge in town was renamed the Thayer Memorial Bridge shortly after his death, decorated with a bronze plaque commemorating him. Mayor Thayer was survived by his wife, Florence Fuller Merrill, and two daughters, one of whom was Ann. Florence's maiden name Merrill provided her grandson with his first name.

And so it was that, in 1946, Whit Rummel Sr., Ann, and little "Bill" drove up to Waterville to visit Grandma Florence for the weekend. Whit wasn't overly keen on spending two days with Florence, but he knew enough to be a good son-in-law. The problem was, he had a lot on his mind, but he wasn't

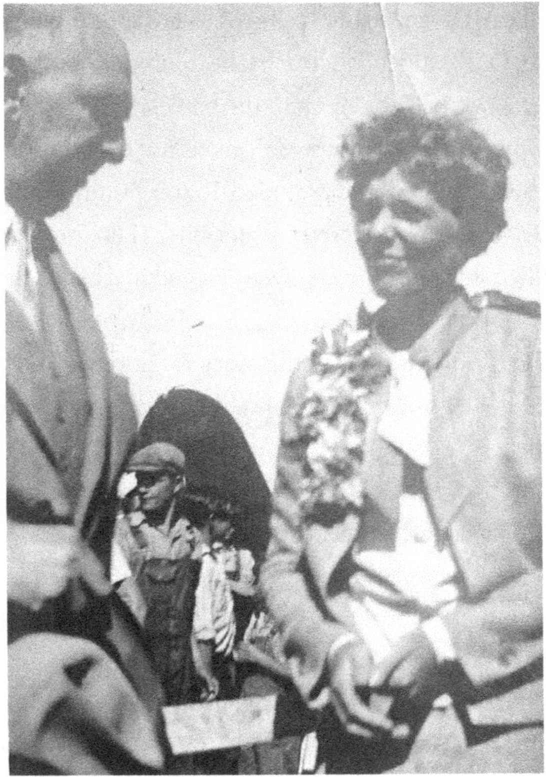

Figure 2.1 *Mayor Thayer with Amelia Earhart*

sure how that weight would shake out. He was looking for that "own thing" of his, looking proactively wherever he went, without knowing what he was looking for.

The morning after arriving in Waterville, Whit excused himself after a breakfast of bacon and eggs and headed into town, telling Ann that he was going for a walk to have a proper look at the place. He'd been there before, of course, for their wedding, so this "proper look at the place" struck Ann as a bit odd—what was there to see that he hadn't seen? But that was Whit, a Seabee full of "Can do" energy who saw the world differently from the way most folks did.

Lunchtime rolled around with no sign of Whit. The meal was served (meatloaf, string beans, mashed potatoes, red Jello for dessert). Still no Whit. Bill went down for his afternoon nap. Still nothing.

It wasn't until early evening that a shiny black Cadillac pulled up in front of Florence's house. Out stepped Uncle Charlie, Florence's brother, though Whit didn't know that when he'd walked into the bank where Charlie was president to make what would be a monumental move for the Rummel family. Then again, of course, a member of the extended Thayer family ran the local bank— the Thayer roots were spread all over Waterville. Then, out of the passenger's side of the Cadillac stepped Whit, his face covered in a big smile that said, "I've just found my own thing!"

Whit and Uncle Charlie laid out the story to Florence and Ann while Bill waddled around the legs of the kitchen table. During his stroll around town, Whit had happened to walk by a defunct ice cream business, the former Webber's Ices. It was *very* defunct—it hadn't been working since before the war, and it looked much the worse for wear after nearly a decade out of commission. A white wooden For Sale sign was hammered into the lawn in front but had been there long enough for the paint to peel and the sign to drift into a diagonal. Nothing a Seabee couldn't fix.

Whit had walked straight from that ruin to the local bank, the name of which was on the For Sale sign. He asked to speak to someone about the property, and out came Uncle Charlie. It was fate.

It was also a good thing it was Uncle Charlie, too, because Whit Rummel Sr. had no savings to speak of, certainly nothing with which to buy the ice cream business. But Whit did give a great spiel. Rhetoric is a gift. Some are trained in it, reading Cicero and attending the debate club. Some just have it in them. They tell the best stories, regardless of whether the content of the story is good—and they'll still keep you engaged even if there's not much meat on the bone. They tell the best jokes, no matter how lame the material. They can sell snow to an Eskimo, the saying goes. Whit had this gift, and it was his primary (let's be honest—at that point, *only*) asset. But he was also in luck, because Uncle Charlie was making the decision, and he knew that his niece Ann had a modest trust fund that had been established by Eugene Lorenzo. It wasn't public knowledge, but it told Charlie that there was a safety net for the bank if Whit's "Can do" attitude in the end couldn't do. He was also happy to do a favor for someone he immediately liked, who happened to be family.

So there it was, Whit said to Ann and Florence at the kitchen table. He'd already signed an agreement to buy the run-down ice cream business. By the way, this wasn't a time when every husband thought it necessary to sound out life decisions with his wife, but Ann was already used to Whit's spontaneous enthusiasm—and it was something she loved about him. And Whit knew that Ann would be happy to move back to Waterville, to her roots, and raise their family there.

So, in a one-morning stroll, the Rummel family's future was set—and they moved to Waterville just a few weeks later.

Whit Sr. needed only a few months to get the run-down ice cream business back up and running. Rummel's Ice Cream was both a parlor, slinging sundaes and banana splits, and a small factory, making the ice cream in-house.

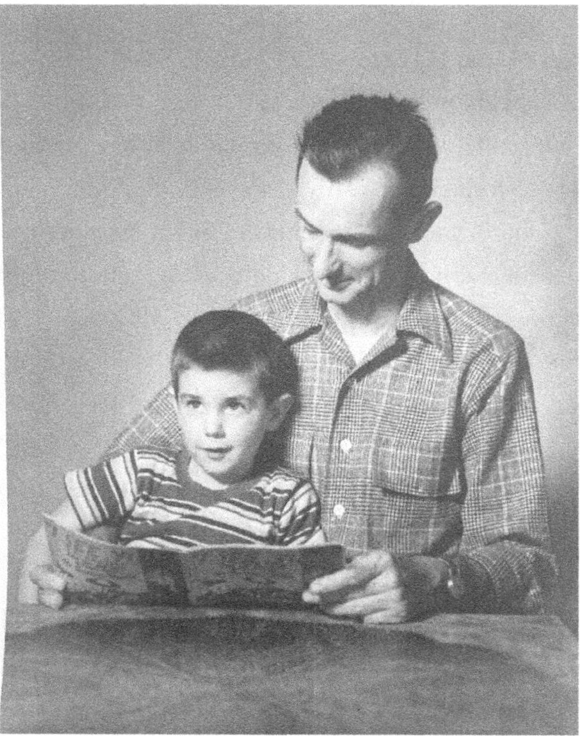

Figure 2.2 *Bill and Dad before I got there*

Whit did nothing halfway, and this extended from his business to the town he now called home. He made sure that he got to know Waterville, and that Watervillians knew him. Rummel's ice cream was good, for sure, but Whit was particularly strong in marketing, generating publicity and great vibes. The day the doors to the parlor opened, he hung a sign out front with the official Rummel's slogan for all to see: "Ice Cream is a Happy Food." He was selling happiness, one scoop at a time.

While it might taste good, no journalist was going to write about vanilla, strawberry, and chocolate ice cream very often. He knew he had to break ground and distinguish Rummel's from other ice cream parlors. He did this by coming up with new flavors with odd, memorable names: Grasshopper, Red Squirrel, Brand X. The one that really took off was licorice. It was ice cream but black as coal, and it truly tasted like real licorice. It made headlines in the local paper, the *Waterville Daily Sentinel*. The article is short, but quoting it gives a good sense of what Whit Rummel Sr. was capable of:

It's Round, Black and Made to Sell Ice Cream

It was black, almost round and was hovering at about 500 feet over the center of Waterville. What was it? Several calls, similar to this one were received at the Sentinel office early Friday evening.

A man, giving his address as Upper College Avenue, near the Sisters' Hospital said he had noticed a dark object that appeared to be suspended over the southwestern part of the city.

Two Sentinel reporters, anxious to learn the identity of this strange objected, journeyed out and soon after beginning travel on Western Avenue sighted an object in the sky.

Watching the "thing" for several moments, they decided to travel back nearer the heart of the city, where the balloon-like object seemed to be hanging.

Meanwhile, streets in the near vicinity were becoming clustered with people craning their necks and wondering what was afloat above them.

Back at the Sentinel office, calls were coming in from anxious onlookers who wanted to know what was "sailing over their homes."

Driving along Grove Street, the reporter decided that whatever the object was must be tethered to something and possibly controlled by someone.

It was found at Rummel's Ices on Silver Street on an almost invisible wire stretching skyward from a tall light pole. A balloon was on the end of the wire.

Determined to find out the complete story, the owner of Rummel's was sought and he was asked the reason for this large black balloon to be floating over his residence.

Whitcomb Rummel grinned. "It's to remind people of our new licorice ice cream," he said.

Rummel had sent up the eight-food in diameter balloon earlier in the evening merely as an advertising stunt. A 15-foot balloon, sent aloft several days ago, burst when reaching an altitude of about 100 feet, Rummel said, but this one did the trick.[2]

It certainly did do the trick, becoming the signature flavor for Rummel's. Whit was just brilliant at branding, and he knew to repeat his slogan, "Ice Cream is a Happy Food," at every opportunity. For instance, he invested in supporting local endeavors, like Rummel's Softball team, which was state champion on multiple occasions, and paid for the state of Maine's first police dog, housed at the Waterville Police Department. He was overtly generous for two reasons: he felt it was the right thing to do, and he saw it as a PR opportunity. The latter doesn't cancel out the goodness of the former. He was a good salesman and a good guy. And whenever he was asked why, he'd repeat the slogan: "Ice Cream is a Happy Food."

The business expanded. In the late 1950s, he installed the first miniature golf course in the state of Maine, right there at Rummel's Ices.

Meanwhile, Whit and Ann had a second son a few years junior to Bill. His name was Whit Jr., and that's me, the author of this book. This is the story of my father, my brother, and an accidental Picasso theft in which I was involved.

3

Waterville, Maine

I was born in Waterville in 1947, the second son and namesake of Whit Rummel Sr. Rummel's Ice Cream had been up and running for a year, and my brother was already three years old. From here on out, since we've now met, I'll refer to Whit Sr. as Dad, so as not to confuse you with too many Whits. (My son is also named Whit, and so is my brother's son!)

I'm the last of the main characters in this story still alive. My dad passed way back in 1972, and we lost Bill in 2015. In order to understand how the Picasso incident played out, how February of 1969 blew up all three of our lives (eventually for the good, fortunately), you need to know the three of us—Dad, Bill, and me—and our dynamic. That means we need to spend a little more time in our childhood, which was ruled by the human being we most admired in the world, our king, knight in shining armor, and court jester rolled into one, the very first Whitcomb Mercer Rummel.

Dad was born on July 16, 1909, in Toledo, Ohio, to Fred and Grace (née Merrill, hence Bill's given name). He was no intellectual but was whip-smart and widely read. He collected coins. He had a prodigious memory that he cultivated—he showed it off by recognizing visitors to the ice cream shop (he and my mother made it a point to remember preferred ice cream flavors too), even if they'd been only once before. He was spontaneous, daring, and decisive. Most importantly, he could make anyone feel at ease and welcome. He'd honed this ability as a traveling salesman when he was a young man, and it served him well.

He met my mother in a cinematic meet-cute. Dad's cousin summered at Camp Runoia in Maine's Belgrade Lakes when she was a girl. During that time, she shared a cabin with another young camper, Ann Thayer. They remained lifelong friends, and when Ann visited the cousin in South Orange, New Jersey. several years later, my dad was offered a date. They must have hit it off because they immediately started living together in New York and eventually married. Dad was selling Birds-Eye Frozen Foods, covering the six states in the southwest corner of the United States, and they traveled together for two years, living out of the trunk of their car and staying in motor courts and hotels while my dad peddled Clarence Birdseye's wares.

When World War II broke out, she waited at home in New York City, while he served in the Seabees in North Africa for four years. When he was finally discharged in 1946, they went off to Waterville to start a brand-new life.

I must say, Dad was a pretty cagey guy and was careful to avoid publicity in his private life. But when it came to business, he sure let it all hang out. In his obituary after his sudden passing in 1972, a friend was quoted as saying, "He also did a lot of things quietly too, you know," implying that the local Waterville *Morning Sentinel* often associated Dad with rather loud and showy PR stunts.[1] A different kind of person with Dad's talents might have eventually run for mayor, and he would've been elected too because he was very popular, but that just wasn't his thing. The most politically active he ever got was when he was made a trustee of the Kennebec Sanitary Treatment District.

No, Dad's realm was his business, which, as fate would have it, happened to be in our very own home.

I remember our house so well. My mother did some research soon after the family moved and discovered it had been there since at least 1820, the year Maine became a state. She tried to look further, but that's when the records stopped. I measured the hand-sewn pine floorboards in my room once, and they *averaged* 18" wide. That would put the date it was built somewhere in the early 1700s. The entire building was a long farmhouse with several other buildings all strung together. Our actual living quarters were tiny: Six rooms, four down, two up, about 1,000 square feet total. The only bathroom was on the first floor, which meant quite a walk if your bedroom was upstairs, which is where my brother's and mine were. Fortunately, we both had easy-to-open windows.

Our heating system was steam, and antiquated radiators, installed sometime in the 1870s, and they clanged constantly in the winter. We had almost no heat upstairs, and all too often the glass of water I'd take up with me at night was frozen over by morning.

I also remember an ancient black slate sink in the kitchen, and I remember Dad showing me the hole at the edge of it, telling me that was where the pump was mounted to get water until they redid the kitchen back in the early 1900s. He was always interested in the way things work; that was undoubtedly the engineer in him.

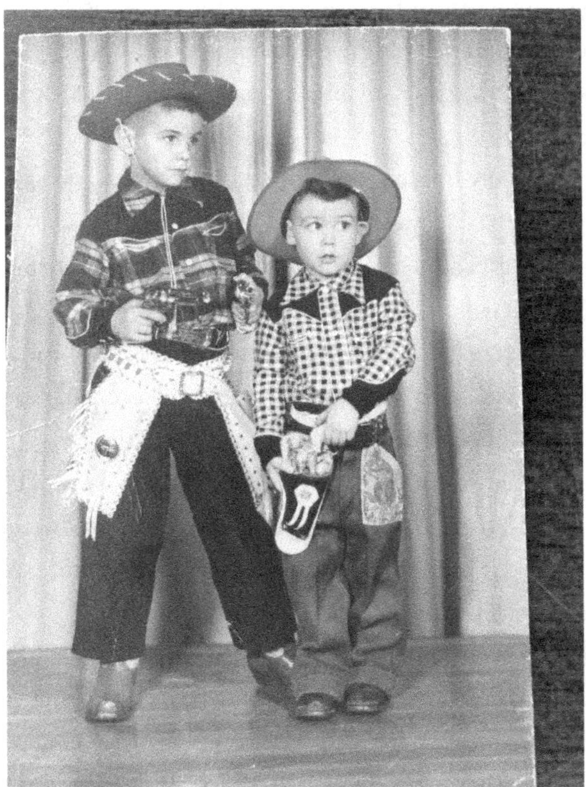

Figure 3.1 *Bill and young Whit as cowboys*

Once you walked out a door on one side of our kitchen, you entered the beginning of all the connected outbuildings: "The Business." It began with the Tea Room, a dining area where customers ate their sandwich or sundae or Icky Orgy. "What the heck was that?" you ask. And that's just what Dad would have wanted you to ask.

An Icky Orgy was a marketing gimmick my father came up with for the ice cream business in the mid-1960s. He set up a showy buffet stand in the middle of the soda fountain, filled with all kinds of sauces, fruits, nuts, candies—anything you could imagine that might go onto an ice cream sundae. First, you'd get a huge bowl filled with five scoops of ice cream with flavors of your choosing, then you could add as many of any of the toppings from the buffet that you wanted. People loved it. Today, make-your-own sundaes aren't so unusual, but as far as I know, this was a first, and Dad invented it. The Icky Orgy outsold the classic banana split by a mile, and when you bought one, you also got a big pin that read "I HAD AN ICKY ORGY AT RUMMEL'S." If you're lucky, you can still find one of those pins today on eBay or some other online auction house—but they'll cost you a lot more than an Icky Orgy ever would have way back when.

Anyway, back to my house tour. Beyond the Tea Room, you took two steps down and entered the soda fountain and ice cream shop. This relatively large room was ringed with counters behind which were the ice cream cabinets that held all the different flavors. Myriad toppings and all the stuff for making malts and shakes and ice cream sodas were located on a central island. This room was always the busiest, and most of the customers ordered from the service windows that faced the parking lot outside.

As you walked beyond the soda fountain, you took a single step up and entered the snack bar. Here, you could order all the sandwiches, hot dogs, hamburgers, lobster rolls, french fries, and a heck of a lot more. Again, most of the orders were placed at an outside service window.

Just beyond the snack bar was a step-up to the manufacturing area. This room had two ice cream-making machines (one ten-gallon and one five-gallon), along with other gizmos for the creation of ice cream bars and ice cream sandwiches. There was always a heck of a lot happening in that room, and it had a brisk, efficient air about it. Often, five or six employees would be hustling around there all at once, me included. By the time I was a teenager, I could do it all: put in the cream mix and different flavorings and weigh the batter so you knew when it was ready. Customers would come in to watch—we always put on a real show—long before the open-kitchen concept in similar facilities was ever a "thing."

Beyond the manufacturing area were the walk-in freezers where all the products were kept. These were relatively large, and there were heavy coats and gloves waiting just outside the doors for when you went inside them. The typical temperature inside was around 10 degrees F.

Beyond the cold rooms, you'd walk up a short cement ramp and there was "the office" where all the "business" was done. It was actually a tiny, cramped area, and I remember the old crank-type calculator for adding up numbers was always cranking away. This was known as Dad's throne room.

At the end of everything was the barn, a truly mystical place with all kinds of serious tools: band saw, table saw, lathe, acetylene torches, and so many other mysterious contraptions Dad would use to repair things or build things. He loved doing that. It was also filled with broken ice cream vending machines brought in for repairs from schools or hospitals that were customers. These needed constant attention, and Dad was the only one who really knew how to fix them.

One of the most amazing parts of the barn was the workbench, a huge old wooden work surface, with three hundred or so hand tools hanging above it for any and every conceivable purpose, and I learned how to use most of them. Finally, there were two huge barn doors that slid open and led you outdoors.

The entire structure, from our living quarters to the end of the barn, was at least 200 feet long, maybe longer, and when I was a kid, the place seemed genuinely endless. It was always an adventure walking from one end to the other, especially in the summertime, because there was so much happening in every room.

Behind the whole complex was a vast open field, first dotted with jumping joint trampolines and later with a miniature golf course.

The only part of the entire place with a cellar was beneath our living quarters. It had a simple dirt floor, and the ceiling, which were actually the floorboards

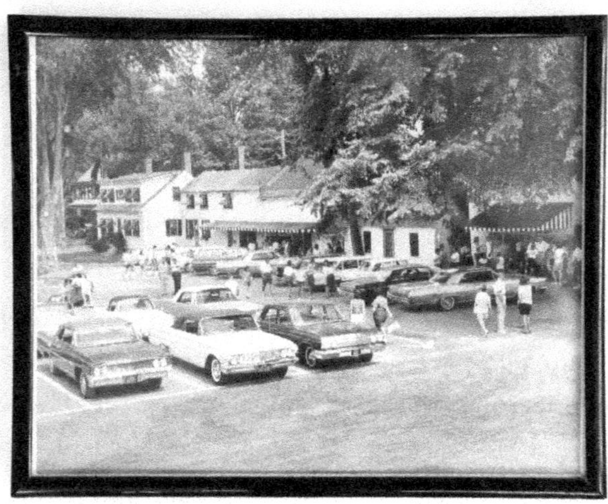

Figure 3.2 *Rummel's Ice Cream 1967*

of the first floor, was just high enough to stand up in. The walls were huge blocks of granite that held up the structure above. Even though the space was relatively small, my father put in a rifle range for my brother, Bill. This range was only about 15 feet long, but Bill *loved* target practice. The backstop was made of a big raw iron slab—a half-inch thick and four-by-four feet square. Dad set it up so it tilted downward somehow, and all of the bullets that hit it would drop harmlessly into a big tray below. Bill became quite a sharpshooter when he was young and won a lot of contests at various junior NRA turkey shoots. He also loved coin collecting to the point of obsession. He picked up the habit when he was eight, and the passion remained for the rest of his life. He knew everything about them: the value, the circulation, the rarity of every US coin ever minted. He'd spend school lunch hours down at the three banks in Waterville, looking through rolls of pennies, nickels, dimes, and quarters. My father was so amazed with his knowledge that he relied on my brother to start his own collection. Over the next decade or so, with my brother's help, he amassed a huge collection, and when he passed away, he very appropriately left it to my brother.

Up in my bedroom, I always had lots of artwork on the walls; one was a reproduction of a painting by Winslow Homer called *The Gulf Stream*. It showed this guy lazing on the deck of a completely wrecked sailboat after a storm, just floating there with all these shark fins swimming menacingly around him. I loved that painting. I also had *The Sleeping Arab* by Henri Rousseau on another wall. A dark-skinned man in this colorful robe sleeps peacefully, with a leopard standing over him and sniffing him. My favorite, of course, was the Picasso I stole from an expensive library book; a print of his painting, *La Celestina.* The print showed a creepy-looking old woman with a cataract eye who, no matter how you looked at her, always appeared to be staring right at you with her one good eye. The image scared the heck out of me whenever I looked at it, and that's why I loved it so much. I *still* love it, as a matter of fact. I've had some version of that image displayed in every place I've ever lived since I first stole it when I was only ten.

I later learned that La Celestina was an iconic character from Spanish literature, specifically the fifteenth-century play *La Celestina* by Fernando de Rojas. Picasso's portrayal, done during his Blue Period (and it is very blue, cool, oceanic, chilling), highlights the old, worn, and tragic nature of the character. The painting features Celestina as a hunched, skeletal figure, conveying a sense of melancholy and despair, but the stare is rock-hard, and the clouded-over eye is monstrous. The muted blues and somber tones reinforce the emotional depth of the piece, capturing Celestina's role as a manipulative, sorrowful character.

My brother's room, on the other hand, didn't have too much in the way of art on the walls. The only things I remember are the many NRA merit certificates he received for his shooting ability. He also had a gun rack right over his bed with two whitetail deer hooves bent at ninety-degree angles; these held the Remington single-shot .22 rifle that he was so proud of.

In a way, the different things we had on our walls is a pretty good way to explain the differences between the two of us. Bill was the "doer," and often acted without thinking things through first. I was more of a "thinker," slower to act perhaps, but more certain of the results of my actions. But more on that later.

Regardless of how different we may have been, we were both in awe of Dad, not only as a dad but as a man who could really make things happen.

Dad also had a macabre sense of humor. And occasionally, it went a lot further than just humor. When I was eight or so, he got together with his best friend, Irving Goodof, the local pathologist, and started The Society of Amateur Physicians and Surgeons—better known as "SAPS." It was made up of two dozen of Waterville's "finer" citizens, and every Sunday, they would have a meeting for two or three hours to discuss "medical stuff."

In reality, I think this was more or less an excuse so they could perform autopsies on a regular basis.

My father always told us that you could learn more about someone from their autopsy than you could anywhere else. So, more often than not, there was an autopsy scheduled. My father enjoyed them immensely. Nothing like an amateur autopsy to look forward to.

But one week, he came back home soon after he'd left. My mother asked him what was wrong.

"You always look forward to it," she said.

But then he answered somewhat gravely, "It's who was being autopsied. I couldn't watch."

"Who was it?" she asked.

"It was Uncle Charlie."

Uncle Charlie was a man my father had known well—he'd been the bank manager whom my father had met with on his first visit to Waterville, who'd let him borrow the money to buy Rummel's Ice Cream.

It didn't take long for that incident to turn into a running joke. That response became a humorous family tradition. Whenever anyone said something like, "You'll never guess who I saw last night . . .," one of us, not just us kids but Mom or Dad as well, would say, "I know one person it *wasn't*." And then we'd all laugh and say in near unison, "It wasn't Uncle Charlie."

Two of my brother's foremost characteristics were his lovability and his naivety. We had lots of Havahart traps when we were kids. Most days, we'd go check on them, often finding a squirrel or chipmunk inside, who we'd usually let loose after carefully studying them.

There was this great garden across the street that belonged to Dr. Bauman, our family physician. My brother had set a larger trap there, not for squirrels, but one big enough to capture a porcupine or something of that scale. Or a skunk, as it turned out. We'd never caught a skunk before, and that was very exciting.

We knew that skunks could get stinky, so with this in mind, we brought the skunk, still inside the cage, back to our house on a beanpole we'd "borrowed" from our neighbor, like hunters returning with a trussed-up trophy. We started to walk through our yard with it, but of course, our yard was also the yard of Rummel's. It was the height of summer, and Rummel's was the busiest place in town, especially right around dinnertime. There were loads of people at the snack bar counter who turned to see us carrying the cage containing an upset skunk as they dined. The guests started leaving in a hurry, and the skunk hadn't even sprayed.

And that's when my father came out to see what we were doing.

Without panicking, but also without smiling, he said calmly, "Okay, boys. In the back. Now."

We skittered into the back and got out of sight. But the customers still seemed to be leaving in a big hurry. I could tell that my father was half-laughing and half-furious and couldn't quite decide which half to lead with. While I could read the scene well enough, though not so well that it would occur to me not to bring a skunk past our family restaurant in the first place, Bill still hadn't put two and two together. He said to Dad, "What's the matter? What the heck did we do wrong?" It's hard to get mad at someone like that. Curious, eager for adventure, to try new things, and with the innocence of a child (even into adulthood). So lovable and innocent, in fact, that it was even hard to get mad at him when we learned he'd stolen a Picasso.

4

Waterville, Maine

I've already given you more information about my father's role in Rummel's Ice Cream than you ever wanted to hear. But truth be told, the Silent Woman venture would truly become his pride and joy. Today, the name undoubtedly sounds somewhat risqué and misogynistic, but that wasn't the thought behind giving the name to a new restaurant in Waterville, Maine, in 1963. Far from it. As a matter of fact, it was a common name in European restaurants, with examples in England, France, Belgium, and Holland. As of this writing, there's still one in Wareham, in Dorset County, England, and another on the Iowa/Wisconsin border. But that may be it because the name doesn't go over so well in today's world, since its origins are just as misogynistic as you might think.

Restaurants and pubs called The Silent Woman have a long and sometimes controversial history, largely tied to an old English tavern sign trope that features a woman without a head or with her mouth covered. The name and imagery originated in the British Isles during the sixteenth and seventeenth centuries and was a part of tavern humor that reflected stereotypical, downright ugly views about women. The notion of a "silent woman" was a jest implying that an "ideal" woman, according to too many people at that time, was one who did not talk back, criticize, or assert herself but cooked really well—an archaic and obviously dated idea.

This trope was visually represented by signage depicting a headless woman, and the theme appeared in various ways: some signs showed the figure decapitated, while others simply had her mouth covered or crossed out. The image was supposed to be both shocking and amusing, playing to an era's darker sense of humor and, of course, is wildly inappropriate by today's standards.

The name was already of questionable taste circa 1965, when Whit Rummel Sr. decided to double down on the success of his first venture in Waterville, Rummel's Ice Cream (originally called Rummel's Ices). It was hugely popular, and Rummel was a marketing whiz.

The back of the menu bore the following phrase: "A Silent Woman-how can that be? Patient Traveler, do not scoff: Drawn from the very life is she and mute, because her head is off." Beneath that, the menu explained the name:

The custom of hanging a sign to attract trade goes back to the early Middle Ages, when only the scholars could read. The tailor displayed a sign with a pair of shears, the hosier a stocking, the inn or tavern, a jug or bottle. The hosts of some inns preferred more original signs, such as The Pig and Whistle, The Mermaid Tavern, The Red Lion, The White Horse, The Bull's Head, to name a very few.

The Silent Woman can be found, surprisingly, by a similar name in France, Great Britain, Belgium, and Holland. The sign probably originated in France as La Bonne Fame, meaning "Good Fame." (The poet Virgil said: "Fame walks the earth, holder her head in the clouds.") It may be guessed that it was changed from "Fame" to "Femme." In England, it is thought that the sign evolved as a satire on Henry the Eighth's method of divorce. Thomas Hardy refers to a Quiet Woman Tavern in The Return of the Native and as recently as 1761 there was a Silent Woman Tavern in Massachusetts.

And so, if you've enjoyed your meal, gentle traveler, please tell of her Good Fame to other northbound hungry persons as she, poor thing, is mute.[1]

There's a lot to unpack in that menu back. The restaurant's interior and the costumes of the waiters were meant to be Olde England-y. Rummel traveled to London to buy antique Vanity Fair prints for the walls back in Maine. But Dad's erudition is evident, at least through my eyes. There's a history lesson in miniature here, a reader of literature (with the Hardy reference), a worn-lightly knowledge of French. And the history makes the name feel more acceptable,

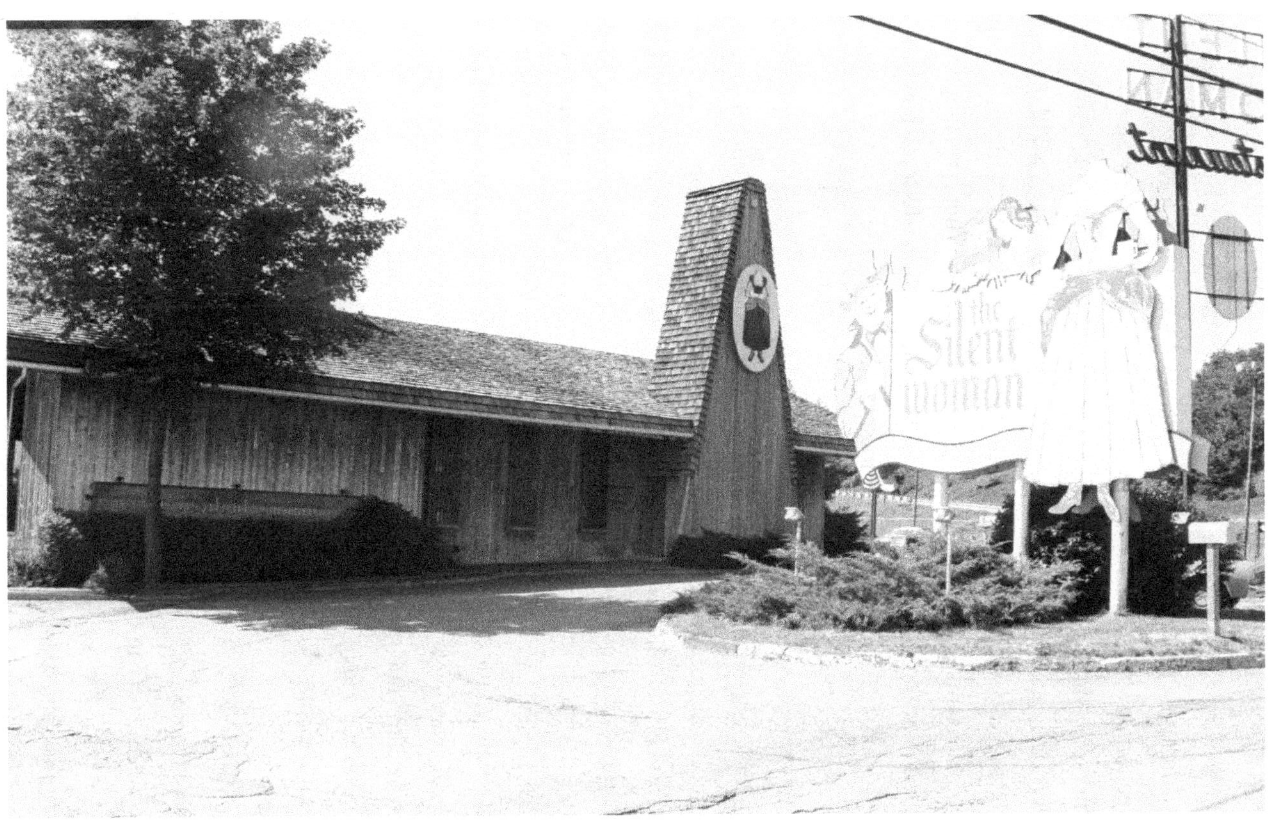

Figure 4.1 *The Silent Woman Restaurant 1969*

even if it is not objectively unobjectionable. As soon as we learn that it is a satire on Henry the Eighth, we can exhale—maybe it's okay to find it funny? Or in today's world, maybe not.

Whatever one's take today, the weirdness worked back then. A Facebook group interested in pre-1980s Maine memorabilia has a glowing chat about recollections of the restaurant. One user recalled [*sic*]: "Never ate there but as a child on summer vacation we got off the Waterville exit and loved seeing it! Loved the façade with larger than life (seemed that big as a kid anyway) woman holding a serving tray with no head. It was the first (and one of the best) advertisement I understood!" Another wrote, "When my folks made their first visit to Maine in 1978 to visit me in Presque Isle from New York, they stopped at the Silent Woman to eat. They loved the whole experience, including the unique name of the restaurant. My father loved to tell the story for many years that followed."[2]

The look received mixed reviews. One user wrote, "Disgusting image even if the food was good," while someone else posted, "I'd be happy to just see a silent woman!! Just kidding ladies!! Chill out!!" Yes, there are all sorts. But the restaurant was his favorite.

Dad advertised in surprising places, but *The New Yorker* was always his favorite. The first ad he ran there read: "Some fine day you will find yourself in Waterville, Maine."[3] He was so proud to see it there that he ran an ad in the magazine every week until he passed away. Ten years' worth. An elite literary magazine like that might seem like an odd spot, but enough *New Yorker* readers vacationed in Maine and passed Waterville "northbound," as the menu says that it became a popular and regular stopping-off point to break up the road trip.

The prices were modest, and the food was, by all accounts, excellent. The chef was Fritz Saul, who had trained in Europe and had been the chef at a restaurant called The Eastland in Portland for two decades before my father recruited him. The restaurant resembled a church from afar, clad in pine, with an A-frame roof sticking up above the main ranch roofline, with a wooden statue of a headless woman fixed upon it. One end of the main dining room was just a giant window, letting light flood in. Architecturally, it was strikingly different and fit right in with the name and story.

I must admit, my father leaned into the weird, possibly inappropriate nature of the name. He ordered plates made of state-of-the-art Pyro Ceram from the Corning factory. White with blood-red details, an ornate design ringed the edges, while a headless woman in a sort of Tudor England-style barmaid dress served food on a tray. The woman's head was very much missing, cleanly cut off at the neck. Text curving above where her head should be read "The Silent Woman" in a Gothic-style font, while curling up beneath her feet ran the words "Waterville in Maine." To her right, three stylized snowflakes. To her left, three crossed knives and forks. The plate served popular dishes like popovers and scallops Nova Scotia, Maine lobster cakes with a "delicate Sherry Lobster Sauce," as an article in *The Morning Sentinel* reported.[4] He was aware that front-of-restaurant etiquette was key, especially for returning customers. His maître d', Naomi Peters, would ensure that customers felt welcome, relaxed, and at home, while both she and my dad made a point of remembering the names and faces of guests and greeted them like old friends when they returned.

The business was Dad's primary focus at all times. Bill and I occasionally felt that we were in second place. But it had always been that way, so for us, it was normal. We acted out as kids, probably no more so than your average rambunctious boys in the pre-video game and -smartphone era, but this may have been due to a subconscious desire to get Dad's attention.

When I was eleven, I got caught shoplifting. A friend and I wanted to see how many colored Magic Markers we could steal without paying. I must have had two dozen or more in my coat pockets and was caught red-handed.

When we went to the police station, my father was called. He made it down in no time, and he convinced the store manager and the police that he would handle it himself—no need for the legal system to get involved. For some reason, they agreed to go along with it. I suppose they knew that Mr. Rummel was a man of his word and that if he said his boy would be disciplined, then he would be.

When we got in the car, I thought I'd gotten off easily, with no police record and no charges. But that was one minute before my father announced what the punishment would be.

As we were driving home, he calmly announced that I was not to go into any store for one full year.

"No store at all?" I asked.

"None," he said.

That turned out to be one of the hardest years of my life. Can you even imagine it? One of the hardest parts was having to wait outside while my mother went into the clothing store to shop for me. I had to try pants on in the car, and it was not fun, believe me.

It may have seemed like a harsh punishment to some, but I sure never shoplifted again.

My father would often pull pranks on us, returning the favor for when we surprised him with our shenanigans. He would take us on "wild goose chases" whenever we had the chance. Sometimes it was just to go to a movie or something, but other times, it was something much more significant.

When I was seven and my brother was twelve, they loaded us into the car on Christmas morning after a rush to root through the Christmas stockings.

My brother and I kept asking, "What are we doing? Where are we going?"

"On a wild goose chase," my father replied.

We knew what that meant: that he'd never tell us before we got there.

We drove all the way to New York, and he never told us where we were going. We ended up getting on a cruise ship. A few days later, we were in Havana, Cuba. For Dad, us not knowing, being surprised, was part of the fun.

My brother and I were running around the hotel in Havana like wild men. A bellhop asked my father if he could show us the machine guns. "It was perfectly safe," he said. This, to my father, was a grand idea. He snapped a photo of us sitting in front of a wall of machine guns. Come to think of it, why was there a wall of machine guns in a Havana hotel?

He was full of adventure, and you never knew when something big might happen. But he was inevitably the instigator, the planner of the adventure. The Picasso heist was perhaps the one time in our family history when we invited him on an adventure, this one of Bill's own, inadvertent, design.

He did other naughty things by design, and to the objective reader, they may not be likely to endear him to you.

Bill had always been a good baseball player and spent most afternoons playing at the sandlot near our house. One day, there was no one there to play ball with, so he decided to play by himself. He returned to our backyard, in the days before a miniature golf course would be installed, and began hitting small rocks instead of balls. He'd toss one in the air to himself, then whack it as hard as he could with the bat.

But you can only whack small rocks with a bat alone at nothing in particular for so long. He grew bored of hitting them randomly and decided to aim at the skylight of a disused chicken coop in a neighbor's yard. Unbelievably, he scored a direct hit on an old window atop the coop, smashing it to pieces.

Later that evening, the owner of the abandoned chicken coop, Mr. Thiboux, came by the house to tell my dad. He was quite upset. My father asked Bill if he'd done it.

"Yes," Bill replied, "I never thought I could actually do it."

Dad then told the neighbor that he'd send a handyman over the next day to repair the damage, and the neighbor agreed. My father gave Bill the benefit of the doubt that night, saying he couldn't really be blamed if he'd accidentally hit one of the windows when it seemed so unlikely to begin with.

The next day, however, Dad's handyman came back from repairing the window. That's when I saw the very concerned look on Dad's face.

He took Bill out back to the barn where all the tools were kept. He took Bill's beloved baseball bat and placed it on the band saw table. He did this slowly, with confidence, ensuring that Bill tasted every moment of it. He proceeded to saw my brother's bat into scores of small pieces. He placed the slices into a large glass jar. Then he made my brother sleep with that glass jar and all the bat pieces for several weeks, the glass jar taking up residence by Bill's bed.

The reason for the abrupt turn of behavior was that Dad had learned from the handyman that there were *two distinct holes* in the same broken window and two small stones found on the chicken coop floor. Incredibly, Bill had actually hit the window *twice*, not just once like he had admitted to. Accident? Maybe the first time, but twice? No way.

A decade later, Bill flunked out of the University of Maine after the first semester of his sophomore year—he was twenty and I was sixteen then. He came home for Christmas break knowing he wouldn't be going back to college. He was absolutely furious at himself and behaving manically. On Christmas night, after presents had been opened and the evening was winding down, Bill told Mom and Dad that he and I were going out for a pizza at Whipper's.

But we didn't go to Whipper's. Bill had other plans that were a bit more self-destructive than a large pepperoni with extra cheese. He got us a couple of six-packs, and we drove around town aimlessly. Around 11 p.m., I asked to go home, but Bill had other ideas. Driving down Main Street, he happened to see a car pulling out of a parking space in front of us. Instead of swerving slightly to avoid the vehicle, he headed straight for it. The driver panicked and reacted swiftly, swerving out of the way—right into another car. It was light as accidents go, but it was entirely my brother's doing.

That moment was the happiest I'd seen Bill all night. He drove on but then said he wanted to go back to see how much damage he'd caused. I immediately begged him not to, that we'd be busted for sure, but he was adamant.

We turned around on a parallel street, looped back, then pulled onto Main Street, where we'd just come from. As I'd predicted, a police car had shown up by then, and when we went past, the driver and his wife pointed us out to the policeman. In no time, the police car caught up with us and took us to the station.

In the detention area, Bill didn't say a word. My brother and I were well-known around town, especially by the police, having been in several mishaps over the years. Nothing properly criminal, but inappropriate kid stuff. One of the policemen finally came in and told us that he'd managed to convince the driver not to press charges if we paid for the damages done to the cars involved and if we also apologized.

My brother thought for a moment, then said, "No way, we'll take it to court."

I couldn't believe my ears. We'd just been given the deal of a lifetime, and he'd refused. Then, ten minutes later, our father walked in. He didn't say a word. He just looked at my brother. Bill immediately did a one-eighty, said that he was sorry and that he'd pay for any damage to the cars.

The next morning, when he and I were on our way over to the husband and wife to apologize, Bill was in tears. Whether it was because he was genuinely sorry or for other reasons, he never said, and it wasn't the sort of thing I could ask him.

The next day, my father escorted Bill down to the enlistment center. First, he tried for the Navy but was turned down because his eyesight was poor. He settled instead for the United States Coast Guard. Was it his choice or was it forced on him by Dad? To Bill's credit, either way, he would embrace it, and the Coast Guard would do him good. At least as good as someone like Bill can be done.

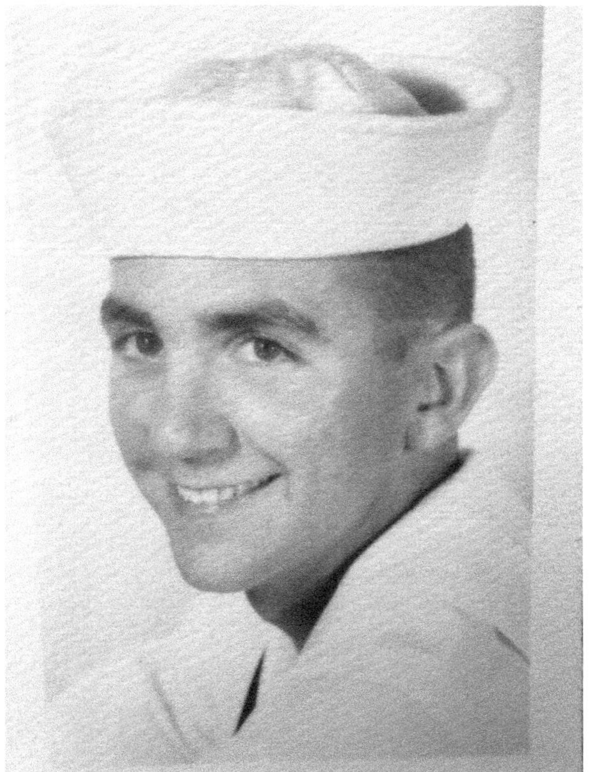

Figure 4.2 *Bill in the Coast Guard*

One month later, he shipped out and eventually became a man, as the saying goes. He certainly grew up, but he couldn't grow out of being Bill. And that's when the fun really started.

5

Europe, 1966

The only valid way for me to receive a deferment was to be in college full-time. And for three and a half years, I was relatively safe. But as my graduation date drew near, I knew it was all coming to an end, and believe me, they wasted no time. In late February, I received a notice to report for a physical only *one week* after graduating. That's right; heaven to hell in no time at all. And I got that notice the very same week that similar, earth-shaking things were happening to Bill *and* to our father. It's no hyperbole to say that the day I got my draft notice was the worst of my life, at least up to that time.

I loved Bill dearly, but in reality, we were as different as night and day. He was all too happy to serve his country instead of going to college. But for me, college was the one thing I'd always looked forward to, a dream I'd had since my earliest days. I couldn't wait to go, to get out of Maine, to learn new things, to have new experiences. When my brother was a kid, his passions were coins and cars, but mine had always been art and literature. I've already mentioned my fascination with Picasso's *Celestina*, how I stole it from the public library. I guess this means both Bill and I have stolen a Picasso—only his happened to be an original.

My father had been very upset by my brother's college "failure." He knew how different Bill and I were, but when I told him I wanted to go to Tulane University, way down in New Orleans, he was not enthusiastic. Our family had some money by that time, but if they had to include extra tuition and travel, that would tip my parents' limit. But with my mother's urging, my father finally agreed to foot the bill if I promised to keep my grade average at least a B or 3.0 every semester for the entire four years. I ended up keeping that promise.

New Orleans was a candy store for this kid from Maine who was looking for something new and exciting. No holds barred and no bars holed. It was the perfect hunting ground for a kid on a quest for new adventures.

That first year at Tulane, I found my passion. It was ART in capital letters and all its forms. I learned more in that one year than I had in all eighteen years before.

Picasso seemed to follow me wherever I went. In my first semester, in one particularly exciting art history class, I saw an incredible documentary about Picasso by the French filmmaker Henri-Georges Clouzot. It was called *Le Mystère Picasso*. I was absolutely stunned because, as I watched, Picasso reminded me so much of my father. He always presented the same sense of confidence and self-assurance that my father had. His incredible ability to make huge, spontaneous, creative decisions was something I'd always seen in my father. After that day, I always equated the two men, long before we were involved in any kind of family heist. It's one of the reasons I've been so obsessed with the whole thing for over fifty years.

When my first year ended, I convinced my father to let me go to Europe to continue slaking my thirst for art. Waterville had some good things going for it, but a lush art scene certainly wasn't one of them. I had enough money for airfare since I'd worked at a gas station in New Orleans throughout the school year. It was the era of hitchhiking, and that would cost me almost nothing. I could stay in youth hostels or just camp out when I had to. Dad even gave me a just-in-case $200, but I never used it and returned it to him upon my return.

It was no surprise that I should have had a wanderlust. My parents created that in me early on. From the time my brother and I were very young, my father would occasionally take us on those "wild goose chases," keeping it a mystery where we were going. These ranged from something as simple as a jaunt to a drive-in movie, a weekend in Boston, a trip to Quebec City, or even a cruise to Cuba. The greatest thing about wild goose chases is having no idea where you are going. I still get excited whenever I hear that phrase. So off I went on my own wild goose chase, certain that I wanted to explore Europe but without much of a plan beyond that. Bill was there too in a way, since he was stationed in Istanbul as part of his time in the Coast Guard, and I promised to visit along the way.

I landed in Ostend, Belgium, in the middle of May 1966 and zipped through a winding route around Great Britain and the continent. I visited dozens of museums: The Van Gogh, Rijksmuseum, El Prado, the Louvre (spending three solid days there), a dozen museums in London and Scotland, the Vatican Museum and its Sistine Chapel, the Uffizi and, of course, Museu Picasso in Barcelona. They were all incredible, and so was every other museum in every little town that had one. If I saw the word "museum," I shot toward it.

I promised Bill I'd visit him in Istanbul, where he was stationed, during my trek, and I fully intended to do so. After visiting Vienna, I traveled to Yugoslavia with the idea that I'd then head east for Istanbul. There, the hitchhiking sucked. I remember walking a full day after crossing the border because there was no traffic. When I got to Ljubljana, I discovered that it was still 1,000 miles from Istanbul. My geography of that part of the world left much to be desired, and I'd somehow envisioned that the Balkans were a great deal more compact than they actually are. Hitching was out of the question in socialist countries because there were so few cars. A Scottish lad I'd met at the border, Stewart, was on his way to Turkey, too, so we decided to travel together as far as Zagreb to see if hitching was any better.

That trip took us six long hours because it stopped so frequently. We decided to get off at Zagreb because hitchhiking would surely be faster than taking this super slow train all the way to Belgrade. But we looked around and saw almost no cars, so we thought better of it. We hopped back on the train and continued. Six hours later, the conductor came through the aisles, announcing, "Ljubjlana. Ljubjlana."

Oops. We'd gotten on the wrong train back in Zagreb and went in the wrong direction, ending up back where we'd started. We detrained, scoped out the situation, and then snuck on a train going all the way to Belgrade because it was leaving right away and we didn't have time to get tickets. We barely missed getting arrested by two menacing policemen who saw us boarding illegally, but the train took off, and we were safe.

In Belgrade, I decided to ditch the idea of visiting Bill. I'd heard Bulgaria was even worse than Yugoslavia for hitching, and Turkey was still five hundred miles away. At the station, I sent a postcard to him telling him I wasn't going to make it, then bought a train ticket for somewhere else.

One of my best moments of that trip was meeting Suzette Gleyses in Carcassonne, France, and travelling with her for a while.

Suzette was so magically exotic for a small-town boy from Maine. She was from a tiny village, Villefranche de Lauragais. She was somewhat naïve, but no more than I was at that time, and she was wide open to adventure. I'll never forget that first night we camped out together in a little park in some tiny, forgotten town. She took off the Greek fishing cap she'd been wearing all day, and suddenly, an endless stream of beautiful, pitch-black, silken hair flowed down to her waist. My God, she was so beautiful. I fell in love instantly. Best of all, she was an artist, studying at the University of Toulouse.

Eventually, we parted, and I continued to Spain—Toledo, El Greco's land, Madrid, and its bullfights. Suzette and I hooked up again in Parmelier near the Andorran border and spent a few last days together before I hitched to Paris and flew home. But I promised I'd return. And a promise is a promise.

From that moment on, I set my sights on returning to France, hopefully to the University of Paris, where Tulane had an exchange program. As soon as I got back to school, I checked what it would take to get there for a year abroad. I immersed myself in French and took the required courses while Suzette and I exchanged romantic letters, dreaming of what we'd do when we got back together. I still have those letters, by the way, and they still mean a lot to me.

I think that Bill was sorely disappointed I didn't make it to Istanbul because, the following Christmas, when I returned to Waterville for the holidays, I received an unexpected gift from him.

It was a live ocelot that he'd had shipped from Guatemala.

It took three full weeks to arrive in Waterville. To top it all off, its container had been sitting outside the downtown Greyhound station for at least one night, maybe more. The temperature at the time was well below freezing at night. The poor thing was close to starving and nearly freezing to death. It was in terrible health and wildly feral. I had to use my old hockey gloves to handle it; otherwise, it would have scratched and bitten me into submission.

What do you do with a wild ocelot your brother sent you as a prank gift?

I took it back to New Orleans with me, hoping for the best. A few weeks later, the poor creature worsened, and I took him to a vet. She took one look at him and insisted on putting him down. I was sad and upset, but the very next day, I woke up with giant rings on my face and over most of my torso. I went to the health service and discovered I had an exotic form of ringworm. It took weeks to get rid of it. I'm sure Bill had his share of giggles over this one, but it wasn't a pleasant experience for me, much less for the poor ocelot.

Midway through my sophomore year, I was notified I'd been accepted into the school's French program in Paris. I was ecstatic. I wrote Suzette and told her. My parents were pleased I'd busted my ass so hard. My father pointed out, however, that I'd have to find decent work that summer to make up for the difference in the tuition fees, which were almost $2,000! I had $500 saved from my part-time job in New Orleans, but where could I find a high-paying enough job to come up with $1,500? I had no idea. A month before the summer break, my father called to tell me a business friend who owned a large construction company had been awarded the contract to construct the new sports center at Colby College in Waterville.

He agreed to have his company hire me for the summer, but I'd have to join the union. No problem with that, I said, especially when my dad told me my wage would be $2.90 an hour. Damn, I'd never made anything even close to that. I agreed instantly. One other thing, my father said. He was going out on a limb to get me this job, and he wanted me to promise him two things: one, that I'd work as hard as I could. No problem there, I told him. I'd never been accused of not working hard enough. And two, that I'd see it through and wouldn't quit. No problem there either, I promised. I *really* wanted this job.

When I got home to Waterville, I started the job immediately. I'd never worked with guys like that—they were skilled career laborers who took real pride in their work. The work was hard, but I was having a ball learning and loved the physical part.

But then, only a couple of weeks after I started, there was an accident.

I was carrying a roofing truss with another guy when he tripped and lost his grip. Unfortunately, I didn't let go of my end soon enough. It cut the last digit of my left forefinger off. And I happen to be left-handed. I picked my severed finger up and wrapped it in tissues. A friend drove me to the nearby Thayer Hospital. Fortunately, there happened to be a skilled hand surgeon there, and he reattached it. He wasn't sure the surgery was going to work and said it could be several weeks before we knew for sure. In the meantime, I had this huge, padded bandage covering my entire forearm. I was no longer able to do the hard work that my job required. But instead of letting me go, the company decided it would be more economical to keep me on. That way, worker compensation wouldn't have to play a part. So, they had me doing menial tasks in the office or just hanging around for show. I hated that so much; guys I'd only recently busted my ass with would come into the trailer and see me sipping coffee or doing stupid busywork that amounted to absolutely nothing.

I felt embarrassed and guilty because I wasn't earning my keep. After a week of that nonsense, I went home and told my father I wanted to quit. He wasn't pleased and reminded me of the limb he'd gone out on to get me the job in the first place. I reminded him that, while he may have gone out on a limb, I may have lost a digit. One thing led to another, and we had a huge argument. I threw some clothes in a bag, jumped into the ten-year-old Rambler I'd bought ($100), and hit the road. It wasn't till I reached the New Hampshire border that I figured out what I would do. I had a friend, Al House, who lived in Delray Beach, Florida, and he was always up for just about anything. I figured I'd drive down there to visit him, *then* figure out what to do next. So that's what I did.

After hanging out on the beach for a week or two in Delray, my finger miraculously mended itself. Maybe it was accidentally getting the bandage wet all the time in salt water. Whatever it was, it healed. Amazingly, it grew back together just a month after it got cut off. It looked pretty weird, kind of crooked and gnarled, and the nerves were screwed up and never did work exactly right again, but it worked just fine. So, we bought a VW hippie van for almost nothing and set off for Alaska, hoping to get jobs because it was salmon fishing season, and we'd heard the pay was fabulous.

Al and I road-tripped up past Anchorage, all the way to Kodiak. It turns out, however, that we'd missed the salmon season.

Several misadventures later, we ended up in Eugene, Oregon, where we bought a beautiful 1951 Cadillac we nicknamed "Hud" after the movie character; we went to San Francisco next. It was the "Summer of Love" there, and we had a ball. Next we went deep into the Baja Peninsula in Mexico before looping back. I ended up back in New Orleans just in time to start my junior year. There was no real rush since I knew I'd lost any chance of going to Paris before I'd even left.

I hadn't called my folks since my father and I had had that argument and left in such a huff. But eventually, I did call home.

They were happy to hear from me; after all, it'd been over three months since they'd heard anything, and they weren't sure if I was still alive. My father didn't harbor any hard feelings, nor did I. From our earliest days, we'd always agreed to keep our word to each other, and when I broke that word, I knew very well what the consequences would be. He might've even agreed with me that taking off wasn't such a bad thing, seeing the choices I was up against. No hard feelings, Dad.

One essential thing I returned with after that incredible trek was a newfound passion: writing. Jack Kerouac has always been my folk hero; I loved how he wrote and his way of describing his wild adventures. However, what *hadn't* appealed to me was the tremendous effort it took for him to write all that stuff down. I was much too lazy to put that much work into it. But when I discovered Brautigan, I realized writing didn't need to be long and laborious. It could be a labor of love. He wrote short and wise and funny and pretty damn deep too, and that's exactly how I wanted to write.

So, that fall at Tulane, I focused all my attention on creative writing and found the perfect mentor. A marvelous man, Professor Husband, helped me immensely with my craft, and I thought I'd finally found what I wanted to do when I grew up.

After my junior year finished, I wrote constantly in New Orleans for the entire summer break. A friend told me she'd heard that Brautigan and one of my favorite poets William Stafford were holding a writer's workshop in Northern California the following summer. I jumped on it and immediately sent a letter telling them how much I wanted to attend. A few weeks later, to my utter surprise and delight, they sent me a very generous response, telling me how much they liked my work and how they were looking forward to my attending the workshop. Talk about seventh heaven.

But then, on February 20, 1969, that dream, and a swarm of others, went straight out the window. Because that's the day I got my draft notice.

The notice told me I had to report for my physical in Augusta, Maine, on May 10 to be inducted into the United States Army. The first thing I did was call the Brautigan workshop to cancel my attendance. But that was only one part of the pain. And I wasn't the only one to receive a shock that February. In fact, the shocks all fell within the same few days that February.

Up in Waterville, by 1968, the Silent Woman had fifty employees and business was booming, so much so that an expansion was planned that would more than triple the capacity, from 80 seats to 350.

It wasn't going to be cheap. The price of the renovation, $100,000 (about $900,000 today!), was oft quoted in the media and was part of the promotion. You should know that one of my father's favorite quotes was, "Why spend your own money when you can spend the bank's?"

As an October 2, 1968, article described, with the renovations underway, "the spot is going to keep running through the changes. Biggest and toughest proposition will come when some of the kitchen apparatus is moved out. When it's finished, Silent Woman will look on the outside a bit like an old English cottage with a roof of redwood shakes. There'll be a banquet area which can be divided into three rooms, another banquet area in the basement, and a cocktail area."[1]

It goes on to say, "Rummel isn't too dazzled by all this—but there's no question that he's proud of the operation." Dad was quoted as saying, "We're not in this for profit. We're putting back the money that we make. I have my ice cream business and Dr. Goodof has his medical practice."[2]

It turned out to be a good thing Dad wasn't in it for an immediate profit because, on February 20, 1969, he got a truly horrific phone call, one that would change the Rummel brand forever. It was the day I'd gotten my draft notice.

The next day, I got a call from my mom telling me about the horrific fire.

Rummel's had burned down.

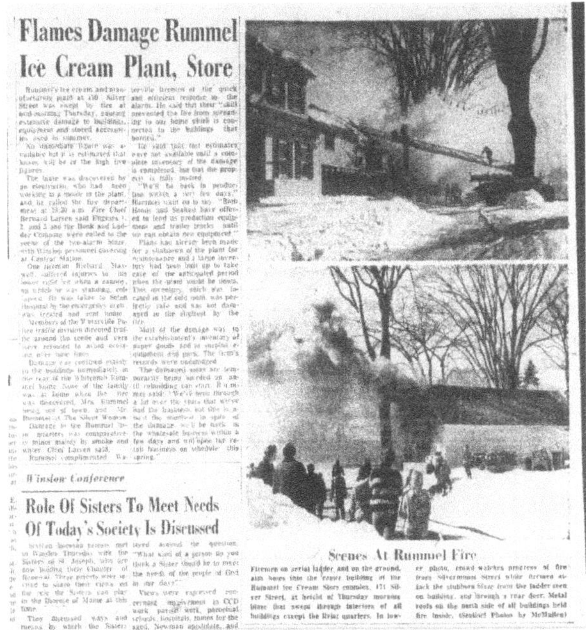

Figure 5.1 *Rummel's Ice Cream Fire Feb 21, 1969. Photo credit Macmullen.*

She was trying not to cry but said the business end of the place was totaled. They managed to save most of our living quarters, but there was a lot of smoke and water damage. I still have some stuff from then and you can still smell the smoke. I thought of my father: sixty years old at the time, his health was kind of sketchy. How the heck were they going to be able to start all over again? I felt so bad for them. I thought it was the end of my world—first, I was drafted, and now this. Goddamn.

But it wasn't over. Fairytales bring things in threes. So does this story.

6

Boston

February 1969

Bill's fingers drummed against the steering wheel of his beloved 1962 Chevy Impala SS as he guided the sleek, pitch-black machine through the Sumner Tunnel. The car purred beneath him, its powerful V-8 engine vibrating under the smooth faux red-leather interior. Snowflakes, just beginning to fall, were caught in the car's headlights, dusting the dark road ahead. It was late February 1969, and Bill was making his routine drive to work. But today, something in the air felt different, as if the city itself was holding its breath.

The Impala glided forward effortlessly, a black bullet cutting through the cold air. On the radio, an edgy guitar riff faded out, and the weatherman's voice cut in, warning of a storm set to slam the city later that afternoon.

"Could be one for the history books, folks. Heavy snow, low visibility. Travel's going to be a mess."

Bill laughed, shaking his head. Boston had seen worse, and his Impala? She could handle anything.

His mind wandered as the city lights flickered above. This was still new to him: Boston, a decent enough job, and a car that turned heads. Just a few years ago, things had been very different. Bill's past unfurled in his mind like a faded film reel.

Bill was fresh out of the Coast Guard, having spent four years in places far removed from the steady hum of civilian life. He hadn't planned on joining the service. His original path had been college—at least, that was what his parents had expected of him. The University of Maine had seemed like a good idea at the time, but Bill quickly learned that classrooms and grades weren't for him. He was the kind of guy who learned by doing, not by reading, and books never held his interest the way engines, stocks, or coins did. He'd flunked out his sophomore year, in 1963, but was that really such a surprise to anyone? Certainly not to him.

His parents were not happy about it, but they accepted the swivel to Plan B. When college fell apart, he enlisted. His father had been a Navy man in World War II, so Bill tried to follow in his footsteps. But the Navy wouldn't take him—bad eyesight. The Coast Guard was the next option, and, unexpectedly, it suited him just fine. He'd grown out of some of his youthful mischief. Service will do that to you. It gives you a solid set of rules to follow and regular habits, which can help the chaotic thrive. He'd worked in supply and was good at what he did. Finding that you're good at something, something that people rely on, is a good maturing experience.

His first assignment was aboard the cutter Dwayne, stationed right there in Boston. Bill had loved the city from the start—its hustle, its history, the way it could be both gritty and grand all at once. His Coast Guard tours took him to places he'd never imagined—through the icy, tempestuous North Sea, to the distant waters of the Sea of Marmara, near Istanbul. Most think of the Coast Guard as just guarding the local coast, but there are tours of duty abroad as well. Adventure to be had.

Turkey had been strange and exciting, yet lonely. The base was isolated, giving him too much time to think and not enough to do. That's when Bill had started playing the stock market, sinking his modest savings into air freight, which he believed was going to be "the next big thing." It was a gut feeling, and Bill always trusted his gut. It paid off, too—his investments grew, proving that his knack for spotting trends was more than beginner's luck. He spent his spare time and stock market earnings collecting coins, an old hobby he'd kept alive since he was a kid. To him, they were more than just collectibles; they were stories, pieces of history in the palm of his hand.

After Turkey came Guantánamo Bay. It was a hairy time, the air thick with tension—Russia's growing friendship with Cuba made Bill's time on the base feel like walking a tightrope. Every day, the threat of something going horribly wrong seemed to hang just beyond the horizon. He'd be lying if he said he wasn't relieved to get out of there.

His final posting brought him to Traverse City, on Michigan's northern peninsula, far from the world's hotspots but no less formative. You can learn a thing or two by tending bar, and he did so at the Non-Commissioned Officers club. The Coast Guard had shaped him in ways he hadn't expected, giving him structure and discipline, traits his younger self had sorely lacked. It was in Traverse City that Bill met Sam. She was a bartender at the bowling alley just down the road from the base, and they hit it off immediately. Sam had a sharp wit and a quick smile, she could mix a mean drink and bowl 270, so he knew she was a keeper. She grounded him in a way few others had.

Bill surprised himself at his success, rising through the ranks and eventually getting to E5, Petty Officer Second Class, which was high considering that he'd only been in the Coast Guard four years. Bill would be the first to tell you that the rank required a combination of technical skill in your occupational specialty—in his case, supply—as well as proven leadership skills, something he never really thought he had but supposed he must. Plus, he had to act as law enforcement, as a federal customs officer.

When the Coast Guard offered him a chance to reenlist, Bill hesitated for just a moment before turning them down. He and Sam were in love and decided to live together once he was out of the service and had found a steady job. Civilian life was calling, who knew, maybe even family life, and Bill was ready to answer.

When it came to a field of work, he had his eye on "the next big thing," the air freight industry. It was a natural extension of his supply work for the Coast Guard, and he'd made a study of it when investing in the stock market, which had paid off. He'd done particularly well for himself by investing in Flying Tiger Line, the first scheduled cargo airline in the United States and the go-to military charter company during the Cold War. This was the company that the US military used for moving personnel and cargo since it was founded in 1945 until it would merge with Federal Express in 1989. It began with a small fleet of just fourteen Budd Conestoga military freighter planes bought as surplus after World War II from the US Navy. By 1949, it was awarded the first commercial air cargo route, from Los Angeles and San Francisco to Boston. It had caught

Bill's eye in 1961, when it became the world's first carrier to offer aerial pallet shipping service. Cargo transport by pallet seemed like the future, and he would have an insider's view in the Coast Guard, especially come 1965, when they started using jets. Jets, planes, cargo, supply, money. It was all his thing. So was Emery Freight, a Boston-based company out of Logan Airport. A buddy in the Coast Guard had tipped him that they were a company to watch, so he'd put some of his savings into them. Between Flying Tiger and Emery, he had more than doubled his investment. All signs pointed in this direction.

He applied for jobs, including one at Emery, the one he wanted most. He got it. He was almost overqualified for the entry-level post, but then again he hadn't gone to college, so that offset his opportunities. But it didn't matter where he began. He would now be working for a company of which he was a partial owner, even if it was an infinitesimal part in the handful of stock he owned. Emery Air Freight beckoned, and so he moved to Boston.

He got himself a room at a boarding house in the Back Bay and started at Emery on the docks, hauling freight and driving forklifts. It wasn't glamorous, but he didn't care. He had a grumpy boss, but who didn't? It didn't matter to Bill: he knew he was going places. The industry was booming, just like he'd predicted, he was now a part of it, and it wouldn't be long before he'd moved up the ranks, just as he had in the Coast Guard. He was a fast learner, and more importantly, he enjoyed it, which can't be said of most work that folks do. Bill had always been obsessed with how things moved, how systems worked. The logistics of air freight fascinated him—the way goods traveled across the globe in hours, how a well-timed shipment could make or break a business.

Things were going well enough that Sam agreed to join him. In early 1969 they rented an apartment on Magoun Avenue in Medford, not far from his work at Logan Airport.

He was building a life, piece by piece. A good job, a woman at his side, a future full of possibilities. He'd long assumed that he would strike it rich—it was just a matter of when and how. He'd been collecting coins since he was nine years old, and that remained a place of optimism for him. He spent a lot of free time visiting coin shops around Boston, hoping to hit a jackpot in spotting an underpriced, very rare specimen that he'd flip for a mint. Then there was his smarts in the stock market, as he saw—not just luck. Whether it was going to be coins or stocks or who knows what else might fall his way, he was damn sure he'd strike it rich. Today they'd call this manifestation. Back then, it was dismissed as wishful thinking by others, but maybe there was something to it?

And then, there was the Impala. He'd picked it up secondhand, but to Bill, it might as well have been brand new. The sleek black beauty was everything he'd ever wanted in a car—powerful, bold, and eye-catching. It turned heads, and when he drove it, Bill felt unstoppable.

Yes, Bill was a high-stakes dreamer. A bit naïve sometimes, a bit naughty, but always optimistic. At least, this was how he saw the world. Never mind that the Impala was seven years old. Never mind that his job was menial and entry-level, and an objective observer would probably think that Bill should be doing better, considering his age and background. Success is in the eye of the beholder.

The tunnel opened up, and Bill merged onto the freeway. The snow was falling harder now, thicker, the flakes swirling like they had a mind of their own. His thoughts drifted back to the weather report, the storm that was coming. He didn't care. Let the snow fall, let the world slow down. Bill was on his way up.

He tapped the gas pedal, pushing the Impala a little faster, eager to get to work. There was something intoxicating about the hum of the engine beneath him, the steady rhythm of the road, the anticipation of what lay ahead. He was on the cusp of something—he could feel it. The years in the service, the hours loading freight, the coin shops he frequented on his days off, the stock market tips he chased—it was all building to something bigger. His hands were cold, but he didn't even think to pull on his black leather gloves.

And yet, in the back of his mind, there was a flicker of something else, a small, nagging feeling he couldn't quite shake but was choosing proactively to ignore. A whisper of danger, of something just out of sight. But Bill had never been one to worry. He was always a high-stakes dreamer, a man with a plan, and nothing—not even a blizzard—was going to get in his way.

Still, a blizzard was predicted. He pulled off the road into a rest stop. The Mobil station sign flickered, some of the bulbs inside on the frizz. He entered the convenience store through a glass door to the sound of a tinkling bell, their attempt at security measures, Bill thought to himself with a smirk. He bought a pack of Camels, then looked out the window. The sky was like a slate tile, the air thickening every minute.

"Gimme four more packs," he said.

The clerk threw them onto the counter. "Don't wanna run short, just in case we get snowed in."

Bill half-smiled, dropped some crumpled bills on the counter, and pocketed the packs. The door tinkled as it closed behind him.

As he approached the airport, the snow began, teasing down in torn-tissue shreds. Bill leaned back in his seat, his eyes on the road ahead, his mind already racing toward the future.

The real storm, after all, hadn't even started yet.

Part II

The Heist

7

Logan Airport, Boston

February 1969

The sky was that soggy, clogged cotton color when Bill pulled his 1962 Impala SS into the employee parking lot at Logan Airport. It was ready to burst, but cold enough that you knew what was coming down.

Emery Air Freight was a big enough deal that it had its own yard, but no hangar. The arriving freight was laid out on a stretch of tarmac. There was no covered storage, which would be a problem in inclement weather.

Bill was one of a handful of employees who did whatever needed doing: manning the forklift, shifting boxes, working the loading dock. There was no union for Emery's staff at the time, but there was a huge dock strike on the East Coast. Bill had heard about it, though he didn't quite understand what it was all about. Freight workers at the Boston docks in the winter of 1968–9 struck, which meant that anything transported by ship was going to have a serious delay. This led to companies shipping goods by air. That was great for Emery's bottom line, but not so great for Emery's overworked staff, which was way behind, with air freight containers full of packages, boxes, crates, and containers piling up faster than they were prepared to handle. Add an impending whopper of a historic snowstorm to this, and you get some funky alchemy.

So when Bill walked into work that February evening—he worked the night shift, 4:00 p.m. to 3:00 a.m. the next day—he just shook his head and wondered if he should've bought another carton or two of Camels.

The Emery section of tarmac was a mess. Air freight would come in from TWA, Pan Am, American, United. They'd have to unload it from the plane, bring it to the tarmac, and sort it out. Some would be loaded onto other planes for new air destinations—Chicago, Los Angeles, New York, and Miami. Others were bound for local delivery. Bill and his colleagues would wait for the right truck to arrive, then load it on, and as the truck pulled away for the next stage in the delivery process, it was time to rinse and repeat. If I'd been the one working this job, I might have called it Sisyphean, but Bill wasn't the literary type to reference ancient Greek mythology about a difficult task that is undone the moment you finish it, forcing you to do the whole thing again.

It was heavy work, too. Air freighters often came in containers that held 4,000 pounds of goods each. There were some forty such containers, and each one was packed with individual crates and boxes. Bill was just twenty-five, but he had a lot to handle in his job. It may sound menial, and it was, but it required sharp focus as well as brawn. He was in charge of outbound items, which meant cataloging freight that had arrived and was due to be transferred to an outbound flight. The originating shipper was responsible for labeling shipments. Bill had to check the labels, sort out international and domestic shipments, which often were dropped in the same pile on the tarmac, identify what needed to move to an outbound flight and when that flight was leaving and get the package there in time. On a good day, with the dock workers allowing freight to move by ship and no biblical weather on the horizon, this wasn't a hard job, nor was it particularly stressful. But tonight? That was a different story, and Bill could feel the tension.

Bill's boss was Peter Mahoney (I've decided not to use his real name because of questions surrounding some of his actions). Mahoney may have been a jerk, but he was the kind of jerk that Bill liked. Mahoney was from East Boston and a veteran, like Bill. Both were working class and proud of it.

Bill checked in and surveyed the chaos. It had been like this ever since the dock workers had gone on strike. Here was a ten-carton shipment, but he could only spot three cartons. Where were the other seven? Production managers from other companies were coming in, some flying in from around the country, trying to locate packages that should have arrived days before but hadn't. Bill was in his work overalls, but Mahoney was catching flak from business types in suits with wingtips plowing through the snow to try to find the packages they were ultimately responsible for in a broken Tetris of cartons on the whitening tarmac. Because, did I mention? It started snowing.

The snow continued for one hundred hours. Nothing moved. Everything came to a complete standstill. No one went home. The pressure on Mahoney had been building, and the steam inside his head was coming out of his ears. The snowstorm had shut down the entire airport. That might sound good on the one hand—time to sort through all the mess of packages—but it would also mean that the piles wouldn't get any smaller as nothing was going out, and the delays piled on the pressure. And speaking of piling up, that's what the snow was doing. The storm hammered in thick flakes toward the crate-covered tarmac.

Bill gave me a play-by-play of what happened next, and, as I remember, it went something like this.

"Bill, what the heck, why isn't the outbound area cleared?" Mahoney shouted, his words kicking steam out of the cold air.

Bill looked around without replying, because everything he could see answered the question for him.

"Well," Mahoney continued, "get it cleared!"

"Most of that stuff isn't even ours, boss," Bill replied. "All those flights diverted out of LaGuardia and JFK . . . "

"I don't care, I've got suits up my ass and snow coming down and trucks friggin' stuck. I just want it gone. Now!"

"What the heck am I supposed to do with it all? It's all outbound but there's nothing going outbound to put it on."

Mahoney rolled his eyes, as if the answer were obvious. "Sort it and set it by the dock doors till the trams are back up. I want it cleared off our plate, and that's that. I don't wanna see jack shit here when I get back."

Then off he stormed.

Bill got to work, not that he wasn't already working, but he hunkered down and sorted as much as he could from his slice of this mess of freight. There was a container of hair dryers. There were cartons of electronics, some partially opened. Each crate or package was different; you'd never know what was inside unless you compared the shipping label to the manifest list, and that wasn't always accurate—it might list "textiles" or "electronics" or "consumer goods"—and labels didn't always stick when exposed to moisture, especially in a massive snowstorm. Shippers were meant to staple labels onto the boxes, not relying only on the adhesive, but that didn't always happen. So some of the packages had partial or damaged or nonexistent labels, and the snow was making it all so much worse.

Bill got as much done as he could. The first night was long and cold and many Camels deep. The night shift ended, but there was no going home. Bill grabbed a few hours of sleep in the office, then awoke and started all over again. The snow kept coming. He did his best, moving the larger crates off to the side, by the dock doors to the terminal, so they were out of the way, at least while they waited for a means of sending them onward to their intended destination. But a pile of crates remained that Bill had no idea what to do with. They were the "orphans" pile. The labels were scuffed beyond recognition or had been torn off. It was an impossible task to figure out where they needed to go without labels, and with the pressure to clear the tarmac, there simply wasn't time or headspace to focus on the orphan cases.

Now, when Bill was interviewed about this same incident by the now-famous Julie Snyder (the creator of *Serial*, for a long time the world's most popular podcast series) for NPR, National Public Radio's "This American Life," he told a different story of what happened next.

He told "This American Life" that, after working nonstop for three full days, Mahoney told him he could take home a few of the crates that had no labels so they wouldn't clog up the dock. One particular crate was two inches thick and three by four feet across. It was substantially different from the other orphans and appeared somewhat "exotic" to Bill. It looked like it had probably been shipped from another country, adding to its allure.

After three endless days, Bill's eternal shift finally came to an end. When the snow was cleared enough to go home, he brought his car around, popped the trunk, placed the crate inside. Off he drove, heading home as best he could through the partly plowed streets, barely able to keep his eyes open.

According to Bill, the crate remained in his trunk for several more days. He'd forgotten about it. Wednesday passed, then Thursday. On Friday, as he was driving home at 3:00 a.m. again from work, he was tuned to a local rock radio station. He was only half-listening, then sat up very suddenly as the radio blared: "Bulletin, bulletin, bulletin. Rare painting missing from Logan Airport." Holy Toledo, he thought to himself (and that I believe, because it's in the transcript from his interview with NPR).[1] At that moment, he told Julie Snyder many years later, he put two and two together and remembered the crate in his trunk.

That's his version, for the record. But I, for one, find that difficult to believe, at least 100 percent. For one thing, I have my doubts that Mahoney actually told him he could take the package home with him. I also believe he opened the package soon after he got it and knew exactly what was inside. It wasn't till after the news broadcast, which was aired in the second half of March, that he suddenly wanted to get rid of it.

He was street-savvy enough to know that such a news report would mean that the police and the Feds would be after the painting. During his second call, I remember him telling me the mob was looking for the painting too, upset that somebody not affiliated with them would have the nerve to steal it. He told me he'd heard it "on the sly" from a local food vendor who catered to the air freight crews.

The radio bulletin said the painting had been reported missing in transit from Logan Airport and that thieves had been stealing Picasso etchings from other places in the greater Boston area as well. It was assumed that these Picasso thefts were all connected.

8

New Orleans

February 23, 1969

I picked up the phone on the tenth ring (this was well before answering machines). I'd been in the shower in my student apartment in New Orleans. The phone was insistent.

"Hi, Whit."

"Hi, Bill." My first thought was that he had remembered my birthday, a small miracle. Turned out that he hadn't.

"You'll never guess what I got."

"You're right, I won't. What?"

"I got a friggin' Picasso!"

Long pause.

"What?"

"I have a real, honest-to-God Picasso painting. And it's sitting on my mantle as we speak!"

"What the hell are you talking about?"

My first instinct was disbelief. What were the chances that three incidents which would alter the spin of the earth under the Rummel family's feet would happen within a period of three days? On February 20, I'd received my draft notice. Later that day, Mom called.

There had been a fire at Rummel's Ice Cream which, if you recall, was attached to our family home. A local newspaper reported damage "in the high five figures," which in today's terms would mean in the high six figures.

The fire had been discovered by an electrician who called the fire department at 10:30 a.m. that day. Firemen descended on a two-alarm blaze—one of them would be injured on the job. The fire was mostly restricted to the ice cream plant part of the complex. Thankfully, no one was there when the fire began, so my parents weren't hurt. They had been off at the site of the Silent Woman expansion, a few minutes' drive away. The local paper quoted my dad as saying that the firemen's "skill prevented the fire from spreading to our home which is connected to the buildings that burned."[1] Thankfully, the property was fully insured. The Silent Woman was still running and expanding. So it was a disaster but not a tragedy. My father was optimistic, even defiant. He told the press, "We'll be back in production within a very few days and will reopen the retail business on schedule this spring."[2] Two rival ice cream companies, Hoods and Sealtest, kindly offered to let Rummel's use some of their equipment and delivery trucks for a time.

If a fire can ever come at a good time, this one did. The ice cream plant was already scheduled to be closed for maintenance and inventory over the winter, when there isn't much call for ice cream anyway, and the snowy conditions helped keep the fire from spreading. The fire had incinerated paper goods and surplus equipment, and to see photos in the newspaper you'd think it had destroyed far more—they show plumes of smoke snaking skyward while a group of onlookers in chunky sweaters stand in the snow, looking on. But the main equipment for making ice cream and the storefront were only slightly damaged. That said, even today, the few pieces of furniture I kept from my childhood home still retain a light scent of smoke.

My parents were staying at the Elmwood Hotel in town until the damage could be fixed. I'd been shocked when I got the call, but honestly, I was so far inside my own echo chamber of concern about the draft notice, and whether I should essentially flee the country to get out of it, that I wasn't as focused on the well-being of my folks as, in retrospect, I should have been.

Still, three days later, this? I wondered if someone had slipped some magic mushrooms into my omelet. It was too weird, too random, to be real. It was probably a prank. The man who shipped me an ocelot as a joke was now slipping me fake news about a Picasso. Maybe he'd found a print at a garage sale and confused it for a real painting? Bill had come up with so many crazy stories in the past, I wasn't sure at the time if this might have been just another one of his tall tales.

I wasn't in the mood for joking around. Not with having received my draft card days earlier. Not with our family's business burned to the ground.

He went on to tell me that there had been a huge snowstorm in Massachusetts the previous week, and he'd been stranded at work at the airport for several days. The airport loading dock was in total chaos; dozens of packages had been lost because the labels had been destroyed during the storm. And somehow (the exact circumstances of which were still in question at that point and remain so to this day), he'd ended up with a "priceless Picasso."

Since I'm telling the story, I'll add here that there was a discrepancy in Bill's story of how he came into "possession" of the painting—there's what I remember him telling me on the phone that day, and then there's what he told Julie Snyder decades later for *This American Life*.[3]

From what I remember him telling me, it was a simple "take." There was no mention of Bill's boss "giving" it to him or somehow allowing him to take it home, much less instructing him to do so. It's important to understand that back then everything was labelled by the originating shipper, not the subsequent go-betweens (of which Emery was just one of several on the painting's intended path from Paris to Florida). Bill had told me matter-of-factly that the package in question had no labels on it, that it had disappeared during the storm, that it was just sitting there, along with several other unidentifiable packages. However, the fact that it was in a solid wood crate and appeared to have been shipped from another country made it quite attractive to him. From what I can remember, he said that he'd simply put the piece in the trunk of his car at some point, without anyone noticing, and that was that. The alternative story, the one that Bill told *This American Life* almost forty years later, is that he was given "permission" to take it. And that it wasn't till several days later that he even *opened* the package to find out what was inside. That, to me, doesn't seem likely.

But however it really happened, he had someone else's Picasso on his mantle.

I mostly listened. After all, what was there to say? The specifics of his story, his tone, convinced me that this was real and that he hadn't been fooled.

"Well, what are you going to do with it?"

He replied with a chuckle, "I don't know. Maybe sell it on the black market."

I scoffed, "What the hell do you know about a 'black market'?"

He just laughed and hung up.

That meant one of two things: that he knew plenty about the black market and I just didn't realize it, or that he *thought* he knew plenty about the black market and was in for a surprise.

Bill's girlfriend, Sam, was away in Michigan finalizing the sale of her house, which meant that he was on his own. Just him and Picasso. The voice of reason was out of town. He was feeling like the cock of the walk. I was annoyed with him. I had my own shit going on, and our parents certainly were knee-deep in it. This wasn't the time to play around with stolen art.

I moved on with my day, worrying about the draft, but his call stuck in the back of my mind like a bone in the throat. I had bigger things to think about. Unfortunately, I couldn't do much about my father's business, but there was a possible solution to my draft board situation.

Realistically, there wasn't much I could do to change my status at that point. Graduation was only a couple of months away, and I hadn't applied to graduate school, so further exemption seemed out of the question as a student. But Canada began to look more and more attractive. If I were to go there, I could avoid the draft completely. It was the main haven for Vietnam War resisters back then, and many thousands of young men decided to take that route. In early 1969, the country announced that it wouldn't ask about an applicant's military status if they sought residence. That was huge.

The downside was that I would no longer be a legal citizen in the United States, which meant any possibility of me ever returning to the United States was just about nonexistent. That was also huge.

I was also in communication with my parents, and their situation seemed pretty bleak. After the fire, our living quarters were still relatively intact, but there was considerable smoke and water damage. To this day, I can still smell smoke fumes on some of the furniture that I have from that time. My parents were temporarily living elsewhere till they could get things sorted out.

All this occupied my mind when Bill called, the first of two calls from him during the time he had the Picasso.

Bill's situation wouldn't leave me be. Part of it was the Picasso connection. Had he nabbed a Monet or a Dali, it might not have haunted my attention. But Picasso was *my* artist, the one I'd been fascinated by since childhood, the one whose print in a fancy library book I had stolen now some fifteen years prior to display on my bedroom wall.

9

Boston

February 1969

It's time that we met the painting in question. Bill would've recognized it as in the style of Picasso, and he'd have seen the signature, but he was no connoisseur nor was he interested in research. He liked the trophy, and that was about it. But as soon as I got involved in the story, I wanted to know everything there was to know about the painting.

Pablo Picasso's *Portrait of a Woman and a Musketeer* (1967) is a very late work that brings together the artist's lifelong experimentation with form and his late-career obsession with historical and romantic themes. Painted during his final decades, this oil-on-canvas work captures both a sense of playfulness and deep reflection. By 1967, Picasso was well into his eighties, yet his energy and creativity hadn't dimmed.

By the time Picasso painted *Portrait of a Woman and a Musketeer*, he was surely the most famous artist in the world (Salvador Dali was a close second), a living legend. He had already revolutionized art multiple times, from Cubism to the emotional weight of works like *Guernica*. But in the 1960s, he was in what some critics call his "late style" phase, characterized by a looser, more spontaneous approach to painting. He worked quickly and prolifically, often completing several pieces in a single day.

This period was marked by a sense of urgency. Picasso was acutely aware of his own mortality, and his work often grappled with themes of aging, love, and legacy. He continued to push boundaries, refusing to rest on his laurels or stick to a single style. For Picasso, every painting was an opportunity to explore, to innovate, and to express his inner world.

The musketeer theme, which *Portrait of a Woman and a Musketeer* exemplifies, was inspired in part by his lifelong fascination with literature (*The Three Musketeers* by Alexandre Dumas was a favorite of his and remained among the most popular French novels of all time) and history. Picasso often turned to the past to find new ways of expressing his ideas, and the musketeer, with its flamboyant attire and aura of romance, became a recurring motif. The musketeer wasn't just a nostalgic throwback; it symbolized freedom, virility, and an idealized masculinity—qualities that Picasso perhaps felt slipping away in his own life as he aged.

The musketeer theme didn't come out of nowhere. In the 1960s, Picasso became deeply interested in the works of the Old Masters, particularly Diego Velázquez and Rembrandt. He admired their ability to imbue historical subjects with life and drama. The musketeer, a figure often associated with seventeenth-century Europe, offered Picasso a way to connect with this artistic heritage while infusing it with his modernist sensibilities.

Picasso's musketeers are also deeply personal. They often reflect his own self-image—aging but defiant, a man grappling with his legacy while still striving to create. They're romantic and theatrical, embodying qualities Picasso admired and perhaps wished to project. These figures also allowed him to explore themes of masculinity and heroism without confining himself to traditional narrative forms.

The painting itself features a seated woman paired with one of these rakish musketeer figures. Her face is an abstract arrangement of lines, shapes, and colors, a nod to Picasso's Cubist roots. Meanwhile, the musketeer is decked out in a broad-brimmed hat and elaborate costume. The two figures seem to occupy separate realms—she is contemplative and grounded, while he exudes an almost theatrical bravado. Their juxtaposition creates a tension that invites viewers to wonder about their relationship. Are they lovers? Figments of each other's imaginations? Or simply symbolic entities coexisting on the canvas?

Portrait of a Woman and a Musketeer is more than just a visually striking piece; it's a window into Picasso's mind at a pivotal moment in his life. The painting encapsulates his fascination with history, his ongoing dialogue with the Old Masters, and his refusal to be constrained by convention. It also speaks to his personal struggles and triumphs—his grappling with aging, his need to assert his vitality, and his unrelenting drive to create.

The woman and musketeer in the painting seem to exist in their own world, yet their presence resonates universally. They remind us of the complexities of human relationships, the interplay of past and present, and the enduring power of imagination. For Picasso, the musketeer was more than a character; it was a symbol of resilience, creativity, and the endless possibilities of art.

This painting, like much of Picasso's late work, challenges viewers to see beyond the surface and engage with the layers of meaning beneath. It's a testament to an artist who, even in his eighties, was still redefining what it meant to be modern.

It would be a while before we learned where the Picasso had come from and where it was meant to end up.

For now, let's rejoin Bill as he stares at the painting on his mantle, trying to figure out both how he got so damn lucky and what he was going to do with this surprise treasure. What he didn't realize yet, but would very soon, is that two different parties had heard about the contents of the vanished crate and were on the hunt for it and whoever took it. There were the police, of course, but also the infamous Boston mob, led by (whom we'd eventually learn) the sinister Whitey Bulger.

10

Boston

March 1969

Bill's situation would have been at the forefront of my mind had it not been for the draft and the fire. I kept wrestling with the idea of going to Canada—one day I decided I would, the next day, not. I went back and forth constantly, but it wouldn't be until I got home that spring that I would finally decide what I would do. Meanwhile, my parents were healing the wounds from the fire and trying to put their lives back on track.

Bill's first call to me was full of cocky bravado. "Look what I got," followed by a sense of omnipotence, that he could do whatever he liked with it. He wasn't the most principled of men but he was not a criminal either, and he knew nothing about the black market or any market, for that matter. But he thought he knew. That's the most dangerous sort of ignorance—the confident kind.

As dramatic narrative would have it, this whole affair coincided with another affair, a cinematic one, that inspired Bill. The original *Thomas Crown Affair* film starring Steve McQueen, Bill's icon of cool, came out in 1968 but Bill saw it in January of 1969, just weeks before the Picasso business. The sequel, starring Pierce Brosnan, is about art theft. The original isn't, but is an iconic film that takes place in Boston and makes slick heists look elegant, something you'd want in your life. Bill saw the Picasso landing in his lap, as it were, as his Steve McQueen moment.

Directed by Norman Jewison, the 1968 *Thomas Crown Affair* is a stylish heist film that captures the sophistication and intrigue of 1960s cinema.

Starring Steve McQueen as the enigmatic millionaire Thomas Crown and Faye Dunaway as the sharp-witted insurance investigator Vicki Anderson, the film centers on an elaborate bank robbery orchestrated by Crown. Using a group of strangers who don't know each other, Crown pulls off the crime with precision, keeping his hands clean and his identity a secret. When Anderson is brought in to investigate, the cat-and-mouse game between the two becomes as much about psychological manipulation as it is about solving the case. Their mutual attraction only deepens the tension, creating an intoxicating blend of romance and suspense.

The film's setting plays a vital role in its allure, particularly its use of Boston as a backdrop. Jewison glamorized the city, showcasing its historic architecture and refined urban spaces, presenting Boston as a hub of sophistication. This is most vividly demonstrated in the sequence at Mount Auburn Cemetery, a serene and lush location that contrasts sharply with the high-stakes criminality of Crown's world. The cemetery, America's first garden cemetery consecrated in 1831, with its picturesque landscaping and Gothic monuments, adds an air of mystery and gravitas to the scene. Its use also subtly underscores the themes of life's fleeting nature and the moral ambiguities of Crown's actions.

The film's glamorous portrayal of Boston extended to the depiction of heists, which were elevated from gritty, violent affairs to orchestrations of elegance and intellect. Crown, a cultured and wealthy antihero, carries out his crimes not out of necessity but for the thrill and challenge, making the heist seem almost like an art form. This depiction influenced a generation of heist films, introducing a blend of luxury, charm, and ingenuity into the genre. Its portrayal of Boston and heists set a high standard for style and sophistication, creating a legacy that continues to inspire filmmakers.

It was enough to make a man like Bill fancy himself a real-life Thomas Crown when a proper treasure came into his hands. He even visited the Mount Auburn Cemetery, imagining himself living a scene like the one in the film. Until the age of ten, Bill and I were being raised as Christian Scientists—I remember when we both agreed that it was a hunk of bunk. But the founder of Christian Science, Mary Baker Eddy, has a spectacular monument in this cemetery, which Bill and I had visited on a few occasions. The cemetery is like a wonderland of landscaping and quirky graves, some of famous Bostonians, others just distinctive—there are many statues of deceased beloved dogs, and there's a sphinx topping another grave. A massive tower punctuates the cemetery like an exclamation point.

Bill engaged in some playful imagining as he walked through the cemetery one clear, icy March day. But his imagination was also toying with him. Or was it?

He was quite sure that a pair of guys in dark overcoats and sunglasses was following him through the cemetery.

He noticed them when their car had pulled into a parking spot on Grove Street just behind his own. They'd entered via the Grove Street Gate before he did, so he didn't think much of it. But then he started to spot them at various points throughout the grounds. They didn't have a camera, which meant they weren't tourists, so they should be visiting the grave of a loved one, he figured. But they were wandering around aimlessly, it seemed, unless their aim was to keep an eye on him. They stood across from him on opposite sides of the Willow Pond. When he'd climbed to the tower up Mountain Avenue, they'd been there at the top and started to make their way down as he arrived. The cemetery is so big that he figured he'd surely lose them if he walked far enough, so he aimed for Halcyon Lake, a good long way from Willow Pond. But they kept popping up.

Bill started to get nervous. Were they police? The FBI? They looked like they might be. Or were they mobsters? Bill had heard that certain members of the "mob" were looking for the painting too, upset that someone totally unknown to them would dare to steal anything behind their back. After all, they supposedly controlled all the illegal activity at Logan Airport. Now someone had gone freelance. No way they were going to let him get away with it. That's where he was in his thinking at the time.

Bill didn't really know what "the mob" was, but if you lived in Boston in the late 1960s, the mob was at least a real, if abstracted concept of organized gangsters who had fingers in many pies, even if you were unlikely to encounter them yourself. It was entirely clear, from the general atmosphere of the city to the winds of pop culture, that you wanted to stay the heck away from any group that sounded like "the mob." He'd heard whispers since he began working at Logan that they were involved in various activities there, but he'd not knowingly encountered them or anyone connected to them. He hoped to keep it that way.

Bill managed to ditch the two men by slipping into the Story Chapel on the far opposite side of the cemetery from where he had parked. It was a hike to get back, but by the time he'd reached his car, their car was gone, and there was no further sign of them. Bill felt relieved but also was on a bit of a high—maybe, he figured, he'd outsmarted either gangsters or cops. But a second thought poured water on this notion, because that would mean that they were trailing him in the first place. He kept checking his rearview mirror on the drive home and was relieved when they didn't reappear.

He had at least one other nervous moment that he mentioned to me. When I'd visit, we used to go to a marvelous, sketchy dive bar called the Hillbilly Ranch. It was incongruous for patrician New England Boston since it was a country and western bar—you'd have thought you were in Texas if you went in. It was located in the seedy part of Boston, known as the Combat Zone. This was the old adult entertainment district, long ago cleaned up. But the Hillbilly Ranch was the place to be from its establishment back in 1939 until 1980. Bill always drank there when he went out, opting for the cheapest beer on the menu, usually Black Label. He was hardly Thomas Crown when it came to taste. There, you could listen to music and dance to acts like the wonderfully named Sleepy LaBeef (a regular), or eat peanuts and throw the shells on the floor. Most nights there was a fistfight or something close to it. It was edgy the way a roadhouse should be.

One night during the latter days of March, when Bill was drinking with friends, he headed to the toilet while his friends waited outside. When he emerged, two toughs were blocking his path.

"You work at Logan?" one asked. Bill's heart dropped a few stories into his gut.

"Yup, I, yes, sir."

"Emery?"

Bill nodded. He wasn't sure what was going to happen next when one of his drinking buddies leaned in the front door and called out to him, "Bill, you comin' or what?"

Bill pushed past the toughs and aimed for the door without looking back. He didn't return to the HillbillyRanch for quite a while after that.

The Picasso was no longer just an anonymous package that no one would notice was stolen. By the end of March, the theft was huge news: it turned out to be a genuine Picasso painting called *Portrait of a Woman and a Musketeer*, made in 1967, and it was worth a fortune. The police had begun to suspect that Emery was its last reported location. Lie detectors were mentioned.

Bill was in a panic. He had no idea what to do now that the painting had been identified and was much wanted. Too much time had passed for him to just give it back and say, "Whoops, I accidentally took this home and forgot to return it." It had been nearly a month, and who'd believe him anyway? Why would he keep a stolen masterpiece all that time? He might get a lesser sentence, but he was certainly guilty of some kind of grand theft. The police were after whoever stole the painting, which meant they were after him. But they weren't the only ones.

11

New Orleans

March 1969

Some three weeks passed before my phone rang again, this time when I was in the shower, yet again. Bill had a knack for timing.

Bill's second call was much different than the first. He was afraid of the police and their lie detector tests, and he was afraid of the mob. And he was probably more than a little afraid of his girlfriend, Sam. She had returned from Michigan and was very upset about the whole thing. Apparently, she didn't like the idea of housing stolen cultural heritage that was wanted both by the cops and the robbers. She wanted Bill to get rid of it as soon as possible.

Which is why he phoned me up.

At that point, as far as Bill knew, no one suspected him. But he'd spent the last three-plus weeks glancing over his shoulder, jumping at shadows, seeing undercover cops inside every collar-up winter coat, and mobsters in every idling van.

After he'd explained his plight in great detail, as I stood in New Orleans wearing only a towel, he asked me the most important question in this entire affair.

"What should I do?"

Instantly, the words came out of my mouth without my having to think about them: "Call Dad."

Our father was, after all, the grand fixer. The one guy who'd always been there for us, pulling us out of whatever kind of jam we'd found ourselves in (and there had been many). Fewer, sure, since we were adults, but I use "adults" in a very loose sense of the word, because we still managed to find trouble, from ocelots to draft cards. His punishments may have been harsh on occasion, but in this case, the various other alternatives were unthinkable. Bill would take Dad's brand of justice any day, when the other options were incarceration or being "whacked" by the mob, as I believe the phrasing goes.

Bill didn't need any more advice from me. I'd told him to do what he was probably thinking of all along. But for all his single-mindedness, he knew that my parents were in a bad spot, and I'm sure that he didn't want to burden them further, didn't want to summon up their disappointment in him, didn't want to cause our mom grief. But this was the clearest way forward, as we had absolute faith in Dad when it came to problem-solving. Bill had what he needed and hung up.

The next day, he called to tell me Dad had listened to his plight. Amazingly, I hadn't been in the shower. Perhaps things were looking up?

"He gave me a couple of choices."

"Choices?" I asked.

"Yeah. I can hold on to the painting if I want to, put it under the new concrete floor they're putting in for the Silent Woman expansion. Leave it there for twenty years or so, then find it, and maybe it would be worth a lot of money, and maybe I'd be able to keep it and sell it legally, and maybe all this hullabaloo will have passed."

I just listened.

"I don't want to do that. I just want to get rid of it and pretend none of this ever happened."

This sounded like my father. He'd always been good about giving us choices. It was never "You have to do this." It was always presented as a choice. Ninety-nine percent of the time, he knew what our answer would be, but it was good to know that if things didn't go the way he'd planned, it was ultimately "our choice." It also helped us grow and take responsibility for our actions. But these were the sorts of lessons best dished out in childhood, when the worst thing you've done is hit a baseball through the neighbor's abandoned chicken coop window. This was rather large in scale, with life on the line.

"What's the other choice?" I asked.

"He said maybe there was a way to return it. Without them knowing who took it."

The phone rang the next day, but it wasn't Bill.

"I understand Bill's filled you in on his dilemma," Dad said.

"Yeah."

Maybe I should have been surprised by my father's next words, but I wasn't really. At least, not if you knew him as well as we did.

"I think we may have a solution."

Wow. Not just thoughts—a *solution*. That's Dad. I kept listening.

"I want you to write a brief note to accompany the return of the painting. Nothing long or complex. Just a few mysterious sentences to put them off the track of someone like Bill."

I understood Dad's implication. From the perspective of the police, Bill was, after all, just a lowly forklift operator. He would be low on anyone's list of suspects to mastermind a heist like this.

"What, exactly, should the note say?" I asked.

That's when he said one of the most important things he ever told me: "I don't know, *you're the writer*."

You're the writer. Did I really just hear that? All my life, I'd waited for him to say something positive about what I was doing. Maybe "Nice game, Whit," when I was in Little League, or just "Way to go," when I made the honor roll in college. But that wasn't the way he'd been raised, so it wasn't the way he'd raised us.

I'd been busting my ass trying to get good enough to call myself a writer, and finally, someone actually called me that. And it was the person I admired most in the world.

Instantly, I was in. One hundred percent. I didn't care if I was going to be an accessory to grand theft or whatever you might call it. This was the closest I could ever remember to having felt praised by my father, and it levitated me.

But Dad thundered forward with his plan. We needed to map out a reverse heist. The painting was already stolen, all too easily, I might add. The tricky part was going to be how to return it without Bill or me, or my father, for that matter, getting arrested or "whacked." Not only would this be the moment when I felt most "seen" by my father, but it was also the start of my part of what was certainly the most momentous and adventurous chapter of my life.

"First thing I want you to do is go to a stationery store and buy some expensive foolscap."

"Foolscap?" I asked. "What the heck is that?"

"It's a kind of paper. That bigshots use."

"Okay," I said uncertainly. "Then what?"

"I want you to buy a pen. An expensive one. An old-fashioned *quill* pen. And some ink."

"Then what?"

"I want you to draft the letter in your off-hand, your *right* one, since you're left-handed. And make sure you write in print, not cursive, so they can't show it to some handwriting analyst and learn stuff about you."

"Then what?"

"Just send it to your brother. Make sure it gets here as soon as possible. Make it Special Delivery."

And that was it.

I hung up and immediately left the Garden District, where my apartment was in New Orleans, destined for an exclusive stationery store. I knew just where it was since I'd passed it almost every weekend on my way to the French Quarter.

Two hours later, I returned to my apartment and got to work. By the time I was ready to write the note, I knew exactly what it was going to say. After trying it out on plain paper a half-dozen times, I figured I had it down well enough down to do it for real.

This is what I ended up with (grammatical quirks are intentional):

PLEASE ACCEPT THIS TO REPLACE IN PART SOME OF THE PAINTINGS REMOVED FROM MUSEUMS THRUOUT THE COUNTRY
ROBBIN' HOOD

I felt delighted with myself, almost insanely clever, in my choice to misspell "Robin Hood" to apply an appropriate double entendre to the note's meaning. If you happened to miss it, that's quite alright. I also misspelled "throughout" to make the note's author look uneducated. I'd left out some commas, too, but who's keeping score?

That same afternoon, I sent the packaged envelope to my brother using Special Delivery, which at that time meant it was delivered to the addressee as soon as it was received at the post office, not waiting around till a carrier delivered it. This made a huge difference in speed, and it arrived the very next day. As I remember, it was expensive—a dollar more than regular air mail. That was a lot in those days.

My job in the actual reverse heist caper was done. I was always adjacent to the unspooling of the crime, with only this one active role to play. But I was a witness and confidante through the thick of it. And the hardest part for the Rummel boys was yet to come. The cops and the mob were closing in. Apparently, the police planned to interview Emery Freight personnel, and the mob was aware of this. So they were going to pay a visit to the Emery staff themselves, in a less formal, more proactive capacity.

12

Boston

March 1969

Today news travel quickly. The internet and cameras in phones in everyone's pocket mean that information has trouble hiding out. But in 1969, that wasn't the case.

In retrospect, it strikes me as amazing to think how slow the process was for the investigation to unspool. Irving Luntz waited literally weeks before reporting that his Picasso was missing. A second artwork, by Alexander Calder, that had also been shipped from France at the same time as the Picasso, arrived on time. Why didn't Luntz report the missing Picasso immediately?

News broke in the *Boston Globe* about the missing Picasso only on March 29, 1969—a month after the incident. The headline, among the many clippings in files I've kept since the event, reads "$75,000 Picasso Stolen at Logan Airport."[1]

A more detailed article, full of speculation, came out the following day as "Case of the Stolen Picassos-International Gang in Hub?[2]" Bill's incident was not the only Picasso-related crime at the time.

The article by Ed Corsetti and Maureen Taylor is short and interesting enough to warrant quoting here.

The chances that an international ring of art thieves is specializing in stealing the works of Pablo Picasso grew stronger Saturday as detectives checked several similarities between two such daring thefts in Boston.

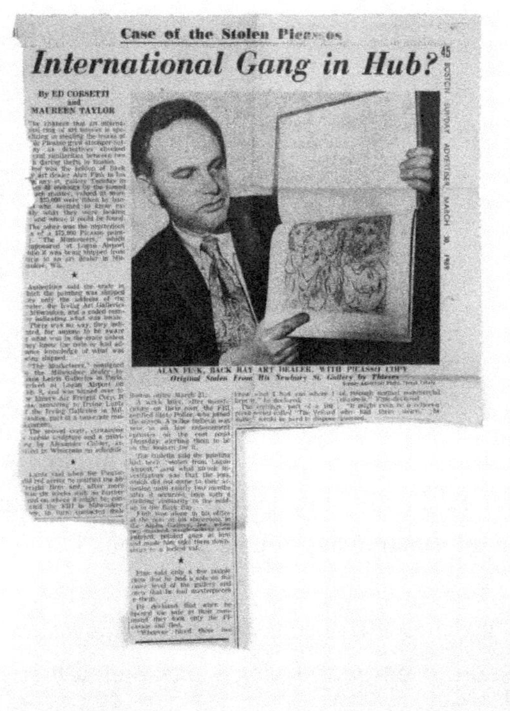

Figure 12.1 *International gang, indeed! Clipping from the Boston Sunday Advertiser. Photo credit: Teresa Zabala*

One was the holiday of Back Bay art dealer Alan Fink in his Newbury Street gallery Tuesday, in which 40 etchings by the famed master, valued at more than $25,000, were taken by bandits who seemed to know exactly what they were looking for and where it could be found.

The other was the mysterious disappearance of a $75,000 Picasso painting, *The Musketeers* [*sic*], which disappeared at Logan Airport while it was being shipped from Paris to an art dealer in Milwaukee, Wis.

Authorities said the crate in which the painting was shipped bore only the address of the dealer, the Irving Art Galleries of Milwaukee, and a coded number indicating what was inside. There was no way, they indicated, for anyone to be aware of what was in the crate unless they knew the code or had advance knowledge of what was being shipped.

The Lady and The Musketeer, consigned to the Milwaukee dealer by Louis Leiris Galleries in Paris, arrived at Logan Airport on Feb 8, and was turned over to the Emory Air Freight Corp. It was, according to Irving Luntz of the Irving Galleries in Milwaukee, part of a two-crate consignment.

The second crate, containing a mobile sculpture and a painting by Alexander Calder, arrived in Wisconsin on schedule.

Luntz said when the Picasso did not arrive he notified the air freight firm and, after more than six weeks with no further word on where it might be, connected the FBI in Milwaukee. They, in turn, contacted their Boston office on March 21.

A week later, after investigating on their own, the FBI notified State Police, who joined the search. A police bulletin was sent to all law enforcement agencies on the East Coast Thursday, alerting them to be on the lookout for it.

The bulletin said the painting had been "stolen from Logan Airport," and what struck investigators was that the loss, which did not come to their attention until nearly two months after it occurred, bore such a striking similarity to the holdup in the Back Bay.

Fink was alone in this office at the rear of his showroom in the Alpha Gallery, Inc. when two masked, rough-talking men entered, pointed guns at him, and made him take them downstairs to a locked safe.

Fink said only a few people knew that he had a safe on the lower level of the gallery and knew what that he had masterpieces in it.

He declared that when he opened the safe at their command, they took only the Picassos and fled.

"Whoever hired these two knew what I had and where I kept it," he declared.

The etchings, part of a 100-piece series called "*The Vollard Suit*, would be hard to dispose of through normal commercial channels," Fink declared. "It might even be a collector who had them stolen," he guessed.[3]

Many such newspaper articles wondered aloud if "a collector" might be behind an art theft in which specific works appeared to have been targeted. This was a common misconception until the early 2000s, when organizations like ARCA (the Association for Research into Crimes against Art) began to study art theft more deeply and learn that commissioned thefts by collectors were so rare as to represent a negligible possibility.[4] But criminal gangs starting in the late 1960s were getting involved in stealing art, because it represented a high-visibility, easily portable, under-secured commodity. There was no specialized knowledge of or interest in art—it was just another stealable for gangsters to add to cars, cigarette smuggling, drugs, booze, and even more grisly things like arms and human trafficking. The first "mob" to become involved was the Corsican Mafia, based in Marseille, in the 1960s. They were especially engaged in stealing Picassos, including a theft in 1976 from the Papal Palace in Avignon, France in which 118 Picassos were stolen. It seems that the Boston mob was also taking note and learning about the value of art the same way the general public was—through television media reports on the extravagant prices for which art sold.

The big sale that caught the attention of the world, criminal and otherwise, came on November 16, 1961, when the Metropolitan Museum of Art bought Rembrandt's *Aristotle Contemplating a Bust of Homer* for a world-record price of $2.3 million.[5] The auction was much covered in the media, particularly on TV, and it helped fix the idea in the popular imagination that art was highly valuable. Criminal gangs would have their eyes peeled for art from that point forward. And the head of the Boston mob was a particularly sharp guy who was likely behind the Back Bay art theft and was likely, decades later, involved in the largest unsolved art theft of all time: the heist from the Isabella Stewart Gardner Museum on Saint Patrick's Day, 1991, when half a billion dollars worth of art, in the form of eighteen works, was stolen. His name was Whitey Bulger.

Decades before James "Whitey" Bulger became one of America's most notorious fugitives, he was a man deeply entrenched in Boston's underworld—a figure whose legend was equal parts charisma and brutality. By the time 1969 rolled around, Bulger had already cemented his place among the city's most formidable criminals. His rise to power in the South Boston criminal scene was as much a story of raw ambition as it was one of calculated violence. His was a name Bill knew, and one he feared.

Bulger had a sturdy build, piercing blue eyes, and a shock of white-blond hair that earned him his lifelong nickname. To those who knew him on the streets of Southie, his appearance belied the ferocity of his character. Behind those calm eyes lay a man of extraordinary cunning, resolve, and a penchant for ruthlessness that would come to define his reign.

Born in 1929, Bulger grew up in the Old Harbor Housing Project, a working-class area where opportunity was scarce and survival often depended on wits. As a boy, he gained a reputation for his daredevil streak and mischievous antics. By his teenage years, he had taken his first steps into crime—stealing, brawling, and running with a local gang. A stint in juvenile detention introduced him to hardened criminals and offered an informal education in the ways of the underworld.

It wasn't long before Whitey's ambitions outgrew petty theft and street brawls. His early crimes reflected his versatility and lack of hesitation in stepping over the line. He was involved in robberies, loansharking, and extortion rackets—crimes that were as much about establishing his dominance as they were about profit. But it was Bulger's sheer audacity that set him apart.

One oft-told anecdote from the late 1950s showcases the lengths to which Bulger would go to maintain control. A rival from a neighboring area tried to muscle into South Boston. Bulger, still in his early days but already known for his temper, didn't hesitate. He tracked the rival down and delivered a beating so severe that word spread quickly: Southie was Whitey's territory, and any encroachment would be met with merciless retribution. It wasn't just the violence that left an impression; it was the cold calculation behind it. Bulger understood the power of fear, and he wielded it expertly.

By the 1960s, Bulger had risen through the ranks of the Boston mob, aligning himself with the Killeen Gang, one of South Boston's dominant criminal groups. He quickly proved himself invaluable, taking on increasingly dangerous assignments that tested both his nerve and loyalty. While many mobsters of the era relied solely on brute force, Bulger combined it with strategic acumen. He cultivated relationships with key figures in Boston's criminal and political spheres, building a network that extended beyond the back alleys of Southie.[6]

His crimes during this period were a portfolio of vice: gambling operations, loan sharking, and drug trafficking. But what truly set him apart was his ability to elude law enforcement. A stint in Alcatraz during the 1950s—where he served time for bank robbery—had hardened him, but it also taught him the value of discretion. When Bulger returned to Boston in the early 1960s, he was more calculating than ever.

Bulger's duality—charming yet terrifying—allowed him to navigate South Boston's close-knit community with ease. He was known to help struggling families in the neighborhood, handing out cash to keep their lights on or pay medical bills. This Robin Hood persona earned him a degree of loyalty and even affection from Southie residents, many of whom turned a blind eye to his darker deeds. But beneath that façade lay a man who would stop at nothing to consolidate power.

One of the defining moments of Bulger's early career came in the late 1960s when tensions between the Killeen Gang and the rival Mullen Gang boiled over into a bloody feud. Bulger's role during this time was instrumental. He acted as both enforcer and tactician, orchestrating hits and striking deals that would ultimately place him in a position of dominance.

Whitey's ability to thrive in chaos was remarkable. He operated with a blend of street smarts and ruthlessness that few could match. His reputation grew, not just as a criminal but as a master manipulator. He cultivated an image of invincibility, using fear as a weapon and keeping his enemies—and allies— off balance.

By 1969, Whitey Bulger was more than just a mobster. He was an emerging power in Boston's criminal underworld, a man whose past hinted at the empire he would eventually build. His story up to that point was one of relentless ambition, calculated violence, and a knack for surviving—and thriving—in one of America's most cutthroat arenas.

The Boston of the late 1960s was a city in flux, and Whitey Bulger was perfectly poised to take advantage of it. His rise to infamy was just beginning, but the groundwork had been laid. Fearless, cunning, and utterly ruthless, Bulger had already proven that he wasn't just another criminal. He was a force to be reckoned with—a storm that Boston would feel for decades to come. Bill was stuck between the law and the likes of Whitey. He had to get rid of the thing they both wanted. It just wasn't worth the risk.

13

Boston

April 1969

As soon as Bill received the note by special delivery from me, he called Dad. Our father told him he'd be down the next day, and they'd carry out its delivery the day after that. Now Dad couldn't come to visit Bill without bringing our mother along, and Mom knew nothing about this. She would've been very upset and her concern would have inhibited the operation, maybe even given Bill away, so she had to be kept in the dark. But she also had to come along to Boston; otherwise, it would have been suspicious.

Bill's girlfriend Sam was all for quickly returning the painting, so she agreed to distract our mother.

When our parents arrived at my brother's Medford apartment, they got busy with their preparations, while Sam entertained our mom in another room. Dad happened to be quite a mystery buff, so they carefully and painstakingly removed all fingerprints and put the Picasso back in its original wood crate. In order to make sure nothing could be traced back to Bill, the outer contents were also wiped down and, after it was cleaned, no one went near it unless they wore gloves.

Claiming that they needed to make a grocery run, Dad and Bill went shopping for disguises. I could imagine the two of them seriously debating the merits of springing for one of those Groucho Marx costumes, with the fake moustache and cigar. Instead, they bought a pair of trench coats—Dad was a Humphrey Bogart fan—and some black felt-brim hats that Bill described as out of "Boston Blackie," a fictional jewel thief and detective created by Jack Boyle in the 1910s, though with a questionable-sounding nickname that would not go over well today. They began as a series of stories published in *The American Magazine* starting in 1914—and illustrated by Bill's Platonic ideal of a great painter, N. C. Wyeth—then were made into films, fourteen of them, in fact. It was an apt reference because Boston Blackie's creator Jack Boyle wrote his stories from Colorado State Penitentiary after having been convicted of robbery—the first four stories were published under the pseudonym "No. 6066," his prisoner ID number. He was a lifetime crook, burgling to support his opium habit. "He lived it, this mystery stuff," Bill said of Dad. This was Dad's chance to literally live it. Whatever concern Dad had for Bill's well-being would have been buoyed by the excitement of it all. He was a man who loved this sort of thing and now could participate in a real-life adventure.

Dad was certainly taking the lead, as ithe had been all our lives. Bill recalled in his interview with Ira Glass, "I thought this is how you do things. He's my father. I'm twenty-five years old. I'm gonna listen to him." Dad had, by this time, been appointed Deputy Sheriff of Waterville, so we both felt assured that he would know what to do, because he'd have a sense of what law enforcement procedure would be. They had to anticipate it to outmaneuver it. They returned with the disguises and a large plastic bag.

The next morning, they packed up my note, but also the painting. The Picasso was back in its shipping crate, both the painting and its box wiped clear of fingerprints and handled only with gloves. Then Dad led Bill in placing the whole shipping crate into the large plastic bag.

They set off with the bagged painting in the backseat of Bill's car. As soon as they got in, Dad pulled out his disguises: flashy sunglasses, a tan trench coat, a felt-brim hat (Boston Blackie style), and an oversized handlebar moustache (Dad couldn't resist, but it was 1969, so oversized handlebar moustaches were not as exotic as they would be today). Bill drove while my father kept a keen lookout for anything out of the ordinary (what could possibly go wrong?). They drove from Medford to downtown Boston and Huntington Avenue, where the Boston Museum of Fine Arts, the MFA, was located. Bill recalled, "He wanted to go in the afternoon, close to closing."

Plan A was to return the painting directly to the MFA. My father had checked everything out on the map, and it seemed a simple matter to turn off the main drag into the parking lot where the loading dock was, with my note attached. This is what was dramatized in Chapter 1 based on the accounts my father and brother told me. But you don't have to flip back in the book, as I'll retell it here.

"Now slow down," Dad said to Bill, "but don't make it look like you're slowing down."

Bill's black 1962 SS cruised by Boston's Museum of Fine Arts. The traffic kept pace for them, with Bill at the wheel and Dad leading from the shotgun seat.

With their disguises, they willfully, gleefully, looked like caricatures of no-goodniks. It was April Fool's Day. Knowing my father pretty well now, you can imagine that this was no coincidence.

Traffic was slow for 2:00 p.m., perhaps because the cold, light rain had driven pedestrians into cabs. The younger man turned on the radio: "The End" by the Doors was just ending.

"It's up here on the left," Dad said. "Turn in."

They wheeled past the Huntington Avenue entrance and around the side before making a quick turn into the museum's back lot. They drove down a slight incline to reach the delivery loading dock, scouting to see if the coast was clear, which wasn't easy since they were both wearing dark sunglasses on a gray, rainy day.

Seeing no one, they pulled into the loading dock, but before Bill could put the Chevy in park, out came three MFA employees, emerging from the building, chatting and pulling out cigarettes, ready for a smoke break.

"Dammit," Dad said. "Get outta here. Go, go, go!"

The cigarettes threw up a smoke screen around the employees, and anyway they didn't seem to notice the Chevy, at least not until Bill hit the gas a little too hard and the tires squealed as the car pulled away.

The Chevy turned onto Louis Prang Street, then onto the Fenway.

The Isabella Stewart Gardner Museum, a misplaced Venetian Gothic palace in the heart of Boston, was on their left, but that wouldn't be robbed for another twenty-one years.

"Pull up over here," Dad said. Bill stopped a block from Boston Commons, just up the street from a swank hotel. An oversized American flag swayed in the chill, wet breeze above the entrance, the words "The Ritz-Carlton" punched out in white against royal blue on the gilded awning. Traffic whizzed past, honking at the Chevy for having stopped so suddenly.

Dad leaned over to Bill. "If I'm not back in three minutes, get the hell outta here. No questions."

It was on to Plan B.

Dad got out of the Chevy along with the painting: and that wasn't as simple as it sounds; in its case, it was three feet by four feet and three inches thick, now in a large plastic bag.

Bill looked on worriedly from the car as his father searched for a cab. He found one in almost no time and approached it. Dad's exact words are lost to history, but the general gist is this: "You want to make a quick fifty bucks?" My father produced a fifty-dollar bill.

The driver nodded eagerly.

"Take this package to the Museum of Fine Arts and drop it off at the loading dock."

The museum was only a few dollars away, so the cabbie was a little suspicious.

"That's it?" he asked.

"That's it," my father replied. He looked at my father's weird getup but then figured, what the hell, nothing ventured, nothing gained.

"Sure," the cabbie said.

My father added, "If you don't do it the way I told you to, I know your name and cab number." Then he closed the door and walked away before the driver could come up with a response.

After waiting for the cabbie to take off, he returned to Bill's car and got in. The next few minutes were tense. As soon as he could, Bill turned the car around and headed down one of the alleys parallel to Commonwealth Ave. He slowed at several stops along the way to allow my father to throw out various parts of his disguise.

That evening, after the initial edge wore off, the two culprits were supremely elated. Sam said this about their reactions over fifty years later when they were watching coverage of the painting's return on the evening news: "They were so excited. Just like a couple of kids. It was like they'd just stolen the painting and got clean away with it, instead of just returning it." I never learned what story they told Mom, who had spent the day with Sam, to explain why they were in such a good mood.

They didn't have long to celebrate together because Bill was due back at work that evening. But a great weight had been lifted off Bill's shoulders, so he practically floated to the night shift.

When Bill got to work, Mahoney came up and told him he had a special job for him. He led him over to a spot and pointed. "See that container in the middle of the dock on that wooden pallet?" Bill nodded. It did look familiar. "Keep an eye on that till it gets shipped out." Lo and behold, it was the Picasso painting he'd just returned.

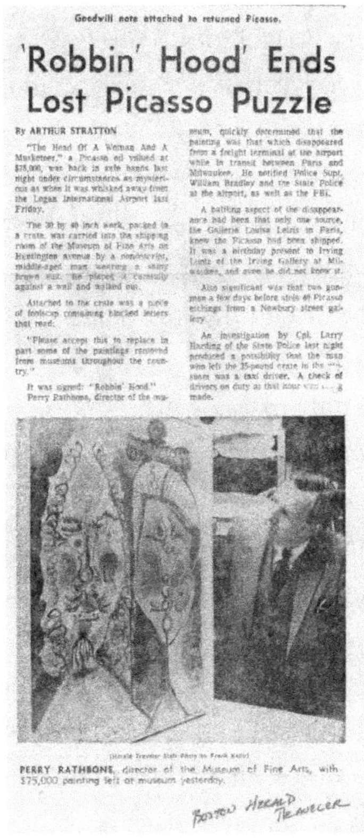

Figure 13.1 *Problem solved! Clipping from the Boston Herald. Photo credit: Frank Kelly*

Bill pretended not to recognize the package. Mahoney continued, "It's the Picasso. They found it." Bill first thought to keep a poker face, but then realized that he needed to react to the news with surprise. "Oh they found it. Huh!"

"It's your job to watch that, seal it up, put the seals on it."

"Yes, sir."

When asked whether Mahoney might have known all along about Bill but had been a good enough guy not to make a thing out of it, seeing as there was a happy ending and all, Bill conceded that it was possible. "Yeah," he told *This American Life,* "a wink kind of assignment." Mahoney knew that he'd taken the crate, but also probably knew that it was an incident of opportunity and that Mahoney himself had sort of encouraged him by saying "get rid of it." So it wasn't out of spite that he assigned him to "guard" the returned painting, but more of an act of solidarity—they'd been in this mess together and thank goodness the mess was past.

Bill stayed on at Emery Freight for twenty-two years, moving from forklift driver to customer service supervisor to operations manager to district manager. He made a career out of it. He finally decided to tell the media decades later, after he and I thoroughly discussed it. He said of this, "My brother and I've never been in agreement on too many things. My mother is ninety-three now [at the time of the interview] and in a nursing home up in Maine. And we thought this might be nice for her to see her boys working on something together. Dad died in 1972."

Bill didn't even know if there was some statute of limitations on his getting in trouble for all this, but since the painting found its way back to its rightful owner, he was in the clear. Still, *This American Life* suggested that they would check on it so Bill wouldn't get into any legal trouble. "That would be pleasant," he said. "It's a rather funny, humorous thing. [Mom] would love it because her two boys were working together."

This was Dad's greatest caper. It was one he didn't manufacture—it fell into his life, and I think he, in truth all three of us Rummel boys, were glad for it. Maybe Dad did manufacture it after all, just not directly? Since he raised us with this caper mentality, turning everyday life into lessons and adventures, we were bound to see what life threw our way in a similar vein.

Dad passed away a few years later. This Picasso reverse heist was a climax to a life dynamically, adventurously lived. As far as I knew at the time, Dad didn't have Adventures with a capital A. He was a traveling salesman, then an ice cream seller, then a restaurateur in a small city in Maine. But his joie de vivre made everyday life an adventure. Until finally a real-life adventure came his way thanks to Bill's quick fingers during the hundred-hour snowstorm.

And that's that, at least for now. It's interesting to note how skittish Bill became because he kept thinking there may have been some way he was going to get found out. For years afterward, all he and Sam wanted to do was forget the incident ever happened and pray they never got caught.

Part III

The Mystery

14

Boston

Spring 1969

My role in the reverse heist was distant but palpable. I'd only written the note, after all. But it felt like an important part of my life, particularly considering the turmoil that coincided with it—the draft, a move to Canada to effectively flee my own country, the Rummel fire. The fact that my brother and father returned it, at no small risk of getting caught, will always be a huge moment in my life. The painting's return, undoing the accidental Picasso theft before anyone got arrested or "whacked" as the local lingo called it, was momentous.

The get-drafted-or-move-to-Canada decision was still heavy on my mind, of course, and the Rummel fire was still a big part of our lives. Returning the Picasso didn't make them go away. But it was like a dose of oxygen among events that made us feel like we were gasping for air. It gave us perspective.

Well, some of us. Bill and his fiancée, Sam, didn't breathe any big sighs of relief. When I got home at the beginning of May, it was still weighing on their minds. For one thing, they were not at all convinced that the law and the mob were done looking for them. They didn't know if, with the painting returned, the case was closed from an FBI perspective, or if they'd still invest resources in punishing whoever "borrowed" it. And would the mob shrug their collective shoulders and move on to the next potential revenue source? Or would they investigate who nabbed a Picasso from under their noses then actually returned it? Of course they would have had a better idea of how to put such a valuable treasure to use. They were still quite scared of being caught, and that's all they could talk about. It wasn't until six months later that Bill and Sam finally stopped suspecting the worst.

In early May, they announced that they were going to get married. Sam had discovered she was pregnant, which may well have sped up operations in this department. According to my later calculations, the date of conception was the same day that Robbin' Hood returned the Picasso. Quite a coincidence.

The wedding was planned for early June, but I barely gave it any thought. After all, I'd been home for a week, and I was due for my induction physical, a step toward joining the army but not officially doing so yet. I still hadn't made up my mind about Canada, when my father did an amazing thing: he told me if I *really* wanted to dodge the draft, he would give me enough money to get a new start in Canada. That took a huge load off my mind. It was also massively selfless of him. If I were to take him up on it, I'd effectively be exiling myself from the United States, which meant I would rarely see him and Mom.

I went to my physical knowing I had this "out" if I opted not to go. Some might report with pride that they passed with flying colors and were told that they were One-A and fit for duty. This did not delight me. I was to report in three weeks' time to begin basic training in the US Army.

Meanwhile, my father had done some research. Of course he had. He'd contacted an old friend of his in the US Marine Corps and was told that, for the first time since World War II, the Marines had initiated their own draft, which meant that they would allow any male over eighteen to enlist for a period of only two years, not the typical Marines' four-year enlistment.

Dad and I decided to meet with the newly retired Marine and drove to China (Maine, that is) to speak with him at his house. He said that there was a huge advantage for someone like me if I were to "volunteer" for the draft. Having already gone through four years of college, he explained, there was no way in hell they'd "waste" someone like me by sending me to Vietnam. I was much too valuable. He was almost certain I'd be selected for some specialized military role in the States. On top of that, I'd even be granted a ninety-day delay if I enlisted immediately.

That did the trick. I decided to join that very day.

Meanwhile, Bill and Sam continued to worry about the possibility of being caught. They had no idea that both the FBI and the Boston Police had abandoned the case as soon as the painting was returned. Law enforcement loves closing cases. They have too many open ones on their desks. If stolen property is found, then the case is shut. But in Bill and Sam's minds, all manner of scenarios presented themselves, none of them good. But now that I'd committed to the Marines, I hardly gave it a thought.

Their wedding was planned for June 12, the day of the grand opening of the Silent Woman's addition. What better place to hold the reception than at the family restaurant? And the party would be held in the very room where Dad had suggested they hide the painting under the floorboards. Had Bill opted to keep the Picasso, then the happy couple's first dance, mere inches above the stolen and incubating painting, would have carried a different meaning. It was certainly for the best, all things considered, that the painting had been returned.

The wedding day rolled around, and seventy-five guests celebrated with a feast at the Silent Woman, followed by extensive partying afterward.

It turned out to be not all that great for me. I'd borrowed one of my folks' cars for the occasion. To make a long story short, my trouble-making days weren't quite over. The evening of the wedding, the borrowed car in question ended up near Colby College, a small liberal arts college at the top of a wooded hill a few miles from downtown Waterville. This wouldn't have been an issue, had I parked terrestrially. However, the car ended up at the bottom of Johnson Pond, while I was escorting a young woman for a "walk" in a nearby field. It's not clear to me to this day what exactly happened, but I suspect it was a couple of "friends" who'd decided to play a rather expensive practical joke.

The police were called, and eventually, a wrecker came and hauled the car out of the pond.

My father was not pleased. It was hardly the ending he'd envisioned for his son's wedding.

The previous day, he'd said goodbye to Bill as he left for the honeymoon. His last words to Sam before they left were—jokingly—"He's *your* problem now." The following day, after the "pond incident," he told me that it would be best to spend the time before my entry into the Marines someplace other than home.

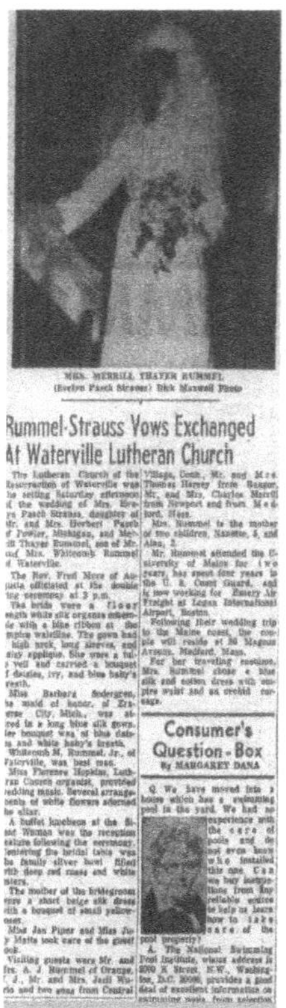

Figure 14.1 *Bill & Sam Rummel's wedding announcement.*

He'd had enough of my shenanigans. In less than twenty-four hours, both of his sons were gone. I didn't blame him one bit.

I drove down to New Orleans, where I spent a debaucherous couple of months before entering basic training at Parris Island in September. I behaved as if I were about to go to prison for a two-year spell which, in my mind, I sort of was, until I learned where I'd be posted.

The Marines came through, though. I wasn't sent overseas. Because I was a "college boy," I was trained in mechanized supply, a crude forerunner of computer processing. It could've been much worse—I was assigned to a Marine base in Honolulu. Duty doesn't get much easier than that. It seemed that being a "college boy" was a good approach. One of my colleagues was even working on a PhD

Waterville News

Car Hauled From Johnson Pond

Local police, firemen, and a wrecker hauled a 1965 Volkswagen station wagon out of 10 feet of water in Johnson Pond at Colby College about 50 feet offshore early Sunday morning and authorities are investigating to determine exactly how it got there.

The vehicle owned by Whitcomb Rummel of Silver Street and being used by his son, Whitcomb, Jr., apparently was pushed into the pond shortly before dawn by two or more unknown male subjects, the unit floating out to a point approximately 50 feet from shore before filling with water and sinking.

Scott Rines of 47 Sanger Avenue, who was parked in a car near the scene, told Colby Guard Al Vieta at 3:15 a.m. that he heard a couple of young male voices shout: "Hey, here's one with no one in it," then heard a splash, and saw the vehicle floating before it sank even though the fog was heavy at the time. He did not see the subjects allegedly responsible for the act.

Vieta passed the word along to local police headquarters by telephone and, shortly thereafter, young Rummel called to report the vehicle had been stolen while he was on a walk around the pond. Rummel said he also heard noises and a splash, but didn't think it was his vehicle involved until it was too late to catch up with the responsible party which apparently jumped into a waiting automobile and fled the scene, so that Rummel didn't get a look at them. He said he left the vehicle parked, ignition shut off, with keys over the visor.

After checking Rines' story with him again personally at his home, police who couldn't see the submerged vehicle until after dawn, called the fire department rescue unit's boat at 4:44 a.m.

After the craft was launched, Patrolman Richard Lane and two rescue unit personnel quickly located the Volkswagen, the top of which then could be seen slightly from shore despite heavy fog.

A fire department diver with an aqua-lung was summoned to go underneath the water's surface and hook on a towing cable when attempts failed to do the same from the boat.

Also at the scene were Officers James Herlihy and Gerald Greene. Winslow Police Officer William Saucier took over the watch when both Waterville cruisers were dispatched on another emergency call.

Figure 14.2 *Submerged auto on my brother's wedding day*

when he was drafted and went on to become the Official Historian for the United States Senate.

The return of the Picasso had been all but forgotten. I had little contact with Bill during that time, and my father never mentioned it. I thought it was over and done, just one more example of our misspent youth.

Little did I know.

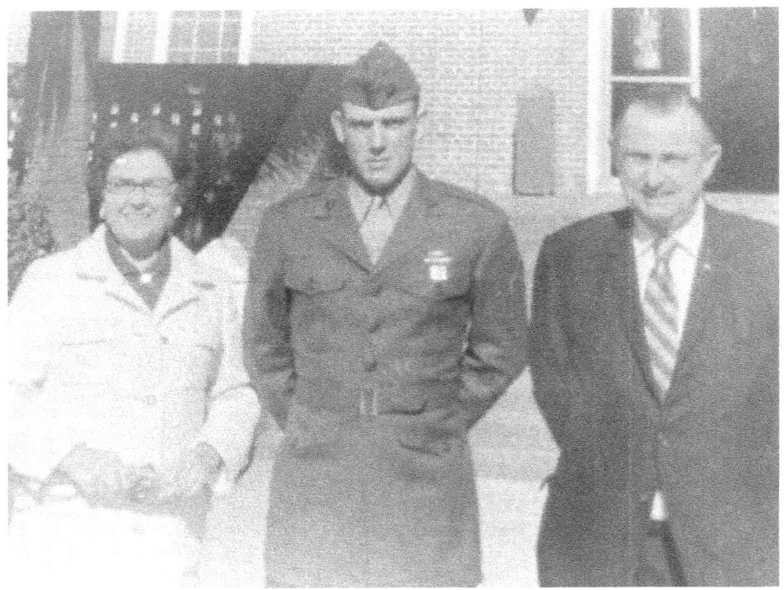

Figure 14.3 *Whit as PFC, USMC, 1969*

15

1971–1988

My parents loved to travel and, as time went on, they spent more and more time doing it. One of Dad's favorite books had always been Jules Verne's *Around the World in 80 Days*. I remember him taking us all down to Boston on one of his wild goose chases when we were kids to see the movie version, with David Niven starring as Phileas Fogg. We watched it in a theater equipped with Cinerama, which I might describe as the IMAX of its time. It was a widescreen motion picture format introduced in 1952 to immerse audiences in panoramic visuals displayed on a deeply curved screen. It offered an impressive sense of depth and peripheral engagement. Though short-lived, Cinerama influenced modern widescreen formats and remains a milestone in cinematic history for its innovative approach to storytelling. It immersed us, as kids, in that film in a way we'd never before experienced.

Fifteen years later, my parents decided to do their own around-the-world-in-eighty-days trip, more or less following Phineas Fogg's trek. Their journey made the local paper, of course, and they had a big sendoff when they left.

They stopped in Hawaii on their return. My father didn't seem his usual self because he mentioned how proud he was of me and my accomplishments over the years. This was weird behavior for him. Weirder still, he told me I was going to be a great writer someday. My father *never* talked to us that way. Something was up, but I had no idea what.

On September 12, 1971, I was released from the Marines, having made it all the way to Corporal. The Vietnam War would fumble on until 1975, but my tour of duty was over. I'd gotten off as easy as one could. From Hawaii, I flew to

San Francisco, then on to Boston. The world was now my oyster, and I could do whatever I wanted with my life. I returned to Waterville very briefly to say hello to my parents, then immediately took off for New Orleans.

Passing through Boston on the way down, I stopped in to see Bill and his wife. The sprout that was still inside Sam when I left for the Marines was now a two-year-old boy named Whitcomb Mercer Rummel, which was my full name exactly, except mine had Jr. at the end of it. My brother had decided to dub him that, not because of me, but because Dad had been so helpful in getting Bill out of the whole Picasso mess. It seemed like a weird gesture at the time. This particular Whit Rummel is a great kid, who is now fifty-five years old as I write this. It's going to get even weirder, too, because when it came time for me to have a son, guess what I named him?

Anyway, when I got to New Orleans, the first thing I did was set up a huge reunion for the guys I'd served with in the Marines. Most of them had gotten out around the same time I did. The big event was planned around Mardi Gras, and it was a smashing success. About a dozen of them came, and they all camped out in my apartment for several days. There may have been a few arrests, as I remember, but not for anything serious. Boys being boys.

At that time, my future as a writer became paramount. I'd had a couple of poems published, along with some short prose, and I was convinced I was on my way. I mean, how could a book about the crazy theft of a famous painting *not* get published?

But then something happened that changed my life forever.

I happened to be up in Waterville for a brief visit, spending a few days on a friend's farm when a state trooper's car pulled up the long dirt road leading to the farmhouse. My friend and I spotted it from the front porch and wondered what the heck was going on. We hadn't been up to any recent mischief that would interest the police. The trooper stepped out of the car. He looked serious.

"Whit Rummel?"

"Yes?"

"I have some sad news."

Dad had dropped dead, suddenly and without warning. Because the farm had no phone, the authorities had asked around for my whereabouts and sent a trooper to break the news.

It's still the worst day of my life.

That thirty-mile drive back to Waterville was endless, even though it took less than an hour. To distract myself along the way, I picked up a couple of young hitchhikers who were more than a little excited when they heard I was heading for Rummel's Ice Cream. They loved the place, they said, especially Whit Rummel, the owner; he's *such* a nice man, they added. I couldn't bring myself to tell them he'd just died; I wanted to keep him alive as long as I possibly could.

When I got home, my mother was still in shock. She sat motionless in her reading chair, unable to speak. My brother was driving up from Boston with Sam but hadn't arrived yet.

Nothing was real. There was no warning, no clue that something like this could happen. He was indestructible, always had been. His absence felt impossible. Yet there it was. My world of carefree sky's-the-limit possibilities had suddenly vanished. An hour later, Bill and Sam arrived, but it didn't help. Nothing did.

In hindsight, he had most likely been ill for some time and never told anyone, not when he came to Hawaii for a visit, and not after I came home. He'd kept it all a secret, just like he did with so many other things in his life.

Hundreds of people came to his funeral. He'd been such a high-profile pillar of the community. But I can't recall much of it. Everything was a blur.

I managed to stay with my mother for four months after the funeral, concerned she wouldn't make it, as she seemed that far lost. But she finally improved, at least enough for me to feel it was safe to leave. I'm still not sure what inspired my next move, but I decided on a brief trip to Pittsburgh to see an old friend I'd known in college.

I ended up staying there, God knows why. I lived with her in her apartment for several months, then bought a place of my own in the Mexican War Streets area of Pittsburgh. In the 1840s, this stretch of land was part of a larger parcel owned by General William Robinson Jr., a prominent local figure who would later serve as mayor of Allegheny City. Inspired by the US conflict with Mexico—then a subject of national attention—Robinson divided his land into narrow plots and named the streets after key battles and leaders of the war: Monterey, Buena Vista, Sherman, and Taylor, among others.

What began as a modest residential development for workers quickly grew into a vibrant neighborhood as Pittsburgh's industrial boom attracted waves of families seeking opportunity. The ornate Victorian homes, built in the late nineteenth century, reflected the prosperity of a burgeoning city. Over time, the neighborhood weathered cycles of decline and renewal, with urban revitalization efforts in the late twentieth century breathing new life into its storied streets. Today, the Mexican War Streets stand as a patchwork of history, art, and community, where the echoes of a distant war are preserved in name, but the enduring spirit of resilience belongs entirely to Pittsburgh. However, when I bought a house there, it was at the bottom of a decline with renewal a distant concept on the horizon.

I bought a three-story brick townhouse for only $15.1,000.

Only a month later, I spent my first night there, alongside a girlfriend at the time named Barbara. We were asleep on a mattress on the second floor since I had just moved in and didn't have any furniture, just a bunch of power tools I was using to fix the place up.

It was about seven in the morning. The windows were still covered in plywood. I remember the pinholes of light streaming in from outside. Other than that, it was pitch dark. Barbara woke me with a little nudge.

"Whit."

"Huh?"

"There's someone here," she whispered. "There are men inside."

I listened. I heard three men mumbling, coming up the stairs. Burglars!

I had no idea what to do. I was in my undies, with nothing weapon-like at hand. I waited, not knowing what to do.

But then, suddenly, I heard my father's voice. He said, "Get 'em!"

I jumped up and shouted as loud as I could, sounding like a madman. Fresh out of the Marines, I was built and intimidating. I scared the shit out of them! All three burglars sprinted down the stairs and out the door. I chased them for

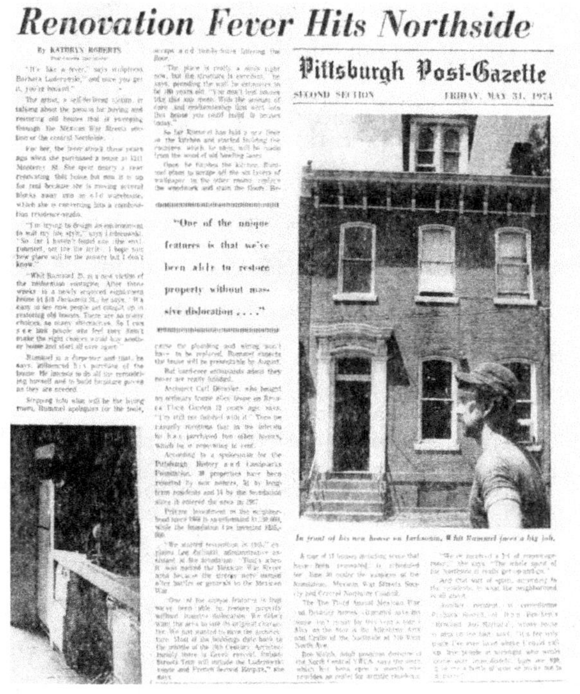

Figure 15.1 *Whit as carpenter, 1973*

a few blocks in my underwear. They'd been after my power tools, of course, which had black-market value, but they were dropping them as they fled.

An old woman was getting out of her car and looked me over as I sprinted past. All I had on was a pair of skivvies. She looked dumbfounded, then pointed in the direction they'd just gone. I continued my chase.

I eventually lost track of the burglars, but I managed to pick up the power tools that they'd taken from the house: a circular saw, a saber saw, a drill. I got all of them back.

By the time I got back, Barbara had called the cops. I was living in an as-yet-ungentrified ghetto, and it would be many more years before it became a lovely place to live. I went back inside my kitchen. Two policemen were there. They and Barbara looked me over.

She said, "Whit, my god."

She pointed to the floor. My feet had been all cut up from broken glass that must have been on the ground during the chase, and there was blood everywhere. My adrenaline was such that I hadn't noticed. A cop there said, "The only way to keep that sort out is to go get a big old junkyard dog." He also said something that should not be repeated in print that was of a racist nature, which I chose to ignore at the time, thinking it best not to correct a cop who had just responded to a burglary on his prejudices.

And that was just one of several times when my father had come to me with advice at the right time. It was truly magical, but I didn't doubt for a second that I'd actually heard it. But that was just the first time. I've heard him speak several times since.

Meanwhile, I had stopped writing completely and did little other than drink and feel sorry for myself. Picasso hadn't reared his head once. And for all I know, I might still be in the dumps in Pittsburgh had it not been for another odd twist of fate.

What finally turned things around was another accident. I'd gone from truck driver to world's worst carpenter while working on my newly purchased house when disaster struck. I was installing a hardwood floor when my utility knife slipped and came within a hair's breadth of cutting my thumb off. The blade severed the *adductor pollicis,* the muscle that attaches the hand to the thumb. It was just flopping there without anything keeping it on except a thin piece of skin.

For a second time, I lucked out at the hospital. There happened to be a hand surgeon on duty who worked diligently to reattach the connector. The prognosis, however, was not optimistic. He sent me home that night and told me to hope for the best but expect the worst.

I still remember that night so clearly: I was in complete despair, knowing I could lose most of the use of my hand and aware that I had no skills whatsoever to compensate. I was sitting on the floor, surrounded by an empty six-pack (or two), when I heard my father's posthumous voice once again. I'm no believer in the supernatural, but at that moment (perhaps spurred on by the six-to-twelve beers and post-operative delirium) I actually heard his voice again. It didn't say anything momentous or life-or-death (though perhaps it would turn out to be).

"Film school," was all he said.

It was so clear and audible. I was sure it was him. Out of the blue, from nowhere. Just "Film school." I'd never even considered that possibility before that night.

It got me thinking. And it made so much sense. From the time I was two or three, I'd always been a rabid movie buff. It was one of the few constants in my life. Without other prospects, why the hell not?

The very next day, with my right arm encased in a huge bandage, I went down to the University of Pittsburgh admissions office and started going through admissions catalogs. I quickly discovered that there were only a half-dozen or so film graduate programs of note at that time, among them UCLA, USC, CalArts, NYU, and Boston University. I took down their contact numbers, went home, and started calling.

It was May at the time, and most schools had already accepted candidates for that fall. I tried the West Coast first. They all said that they weren't accepting applications at that time and I should inquire later in the year. NYU said the same thing. Finally, I tried Boston University, the last East Coast college at the time with a graduate program in film. I was connected to George Bluestone, head of the graduate program. He listened to my plea and, for some reason, still hazy to this day, he agreed to see me in person to talk about it. He had no idea, of course, that I was in Pittsburgh, but that didn't make a difference. I scheduled an appointment for later that week, then got in my car and drove 600 miles to Boston to meet him.

The meeting was magical. There I was, my right hand and most of my forearm completely covered in thick bandages, talking about how important film school was and how I just *had* to get in as soon as possible. He said no at first, but when he recognized how important it was to me, he said there just might be a possibility of starting with non-production classes first, then taking production in the fall.

In my father's will, he left me only a modest share in an apartment, which I sold for a few thousand bucks soon after to help with grad school. The older I've gotten, the more I appreciate his wisdom in letting me make my own way in the world and not be dependent on his good fortune.

All roads seemed to lead to Boston. As the lyrics of "Dirty Water" go, "Boston you're my home." I haven't had a day since when I wasn't happy about the career I chose.

For the next several years, the Picasso theft was all but forgotten. I'd occasionally dream of making a movie out of it, because I thought it was such a wonderful story. But I was much too busy with my career.

After grad school, I spent the better part of a year on the oil rigs in the Saudi Arabia desert, shooting a series of instructional films. Then I started a company called WITCOM (observant readers will recognize the pun on my name), which specialized in high-end corporate films (actually, it was mostly video then). We happened to come along at just the right time and became quite successful.

This went on until 1988, when I decided I'd had enough. The company had grown so large that I ended up spending more and more time managing and less and less time filmmaking. On April 1 (the date has long been a traditional one for big events in our family), I sold the company. It was bought by another,

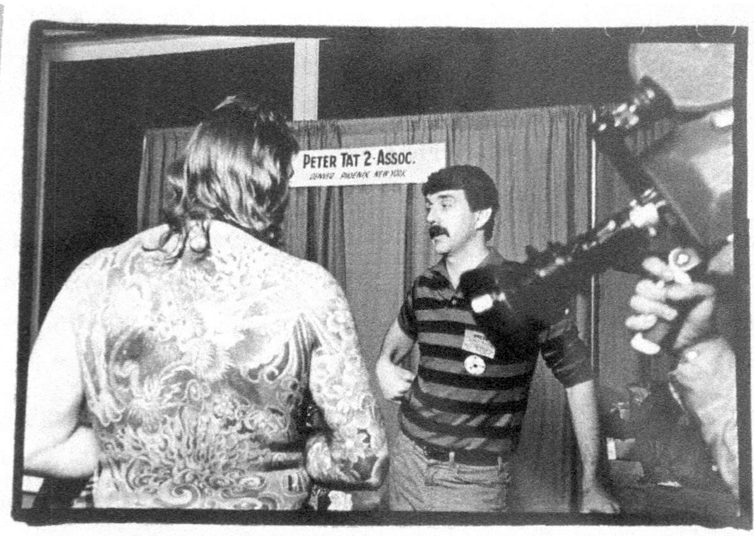

Figure 15.2 *Whit as filmmaker, 1978*

larger company in the same kind of business. It lived on successfully, and it was a great deal financially. I agreed to stay on as a partner. It was one of the many times I wished my father hadn't died so early; I think he'd have been proud of me.

I was forty-one years old, financially solid, doing what I liked and sufficiently empowered to stop when I wished to. As soon as I sold, I thought of marriage for the first time. Six months later, I married a wonderful woman who, miraculously, is still my wife. And exactly nine months later, we had a son, whom we decided to name Whit. Yes, if you've been keeping score, that's the fourth Whitcomb Rummel to appear within three generations. It can make it confusing sometimes when opening gifts on Christmas morning, but we've always managed somehow.

I suddenly had a future that included more than myself, and it was very exciting.

On my son's first birthday, I was late getting to his party because we were having a WARP party at WITCOM, where I was now a partner. WARP was a variant of a "wrap" party, an inside joke that stood for the "Witcom Alcohol Rehabilitation Program." Most Fridays, we'd have an after-work get-together involving a case or two of beer.

I had a little buzz on by the time I got home and gave young Whit a big, boisterous hello. He looked at me curiously from his high-chair and didn't immediately respond. He just stared at me. At that very moment, I heard a voice say, clear as a bell, "That's enough."

There was no one around but the two of us. It was clearly my father's voice again, and it was several years after his passing. I *know* I heard it.

I haven't had a drop of liquor since that moment. It's been thirty-five years as I write, and it's been one of the best decisions I ever made.

Dad would present me with yet another huge surprise. And that's when Picasso would come flooding back into my life.

16

Waterville, Maine

1994

In early 1994, my wife, son, and I were in Waterville visiting my mother for a few days. One afternoon, I was up in the attic, looking for who knows what. The attic was dusty and musty and full of cardboard boxes of clothes no one would wear, empty picture frames, orphaned lampshades, the sort of bric-a-brac that builds up over time and never gets sorted unless someone passes away.

While looking for something else entirely, I happened to find an old wooden chest that I'd never seen before. It turned out that it had belonged to my father when he was a child. The chest had been sent to my mother a few years earlier upon the death of one of my father's relatives.

I should repeat here that my father had *never* mentioned anything about his life before he was married. Not once, ever.

When I opened that chest, I discovered, for the very first time, what had happened during the first twenty years of my father's life.

Perhaps what surprised me most was learning that his birth mother had died, suddenly, when he was nine years old. According to the baby album that was in the chest, the first years were very happy indeed. Dozens of photos, from infancy to age nine, were meticulously kept. It was obvious that he and his mother were very close. But then, right around Christmas 1918, the memories stopped. I looked through documents and discovered that his mother had died in the Spanish Flu epidemic of 1918. One day she'd been perfectly fit and healthy, but within just a few days, she was dead.

How terrible that must have been. I explored the chest further and discovered that, two months after her death, he had been abandoned by his father, who had decided to move from their home in Ohio to New Jersey, by himself, for reasons unknown. His father sold the family home, and Dad and his younger brother were sent to live with three maiden aunts. There was certainly no love lost there, judging from the plentiful plaintive letters he'd sent to his father. He continually asked if he could move East to be with him, but it never happened. The chest did not contain an answer to the looming question—why, how on earth, could a father abandon his young sons just after their mother suddenly died? As a father myself, I couldn't fathom it. Times were different, I guess.

Dad was seventeen when he left that unhappy abode, leaving his sisters behind and setting off on his own.

First, he got a job (having falsified his birth date to qualify) as a stevedore on a freighter for six months, sailing around Cape Horn and beyond. Next, he moved to Manhattan, where he began his acting career. He received his Actors Equity card and got several parts in plays. He spent a couple of years at it, actually eking out a living, but then, for one reason or another, moved on to other things.

Imagine my amazement at each of these revelations. What? My dad had been a professional actor? He was abandoned? Out of the chest flew surprise after surprise, and it would take time for each one, like pieces in a puzzle, to drift into place, filling out my understanding of the most influential person in my life, who was no longer there to tell the stories and clearly had never wanted them told in the first place.

Here was the new father I'd never known. No wonder he'd had so much fun playing the role of Robbin' Hood during the return of the Picasso. He stretched his acting wings for the first time in decades.

I spent the entire afternoon acquainting myself with a dad I hadn't known. There was much crying involved. When I finally came downstairs to join my wife and son, I was a different person.

To celebrate the occasion, I came up with a unique plan. On April 1, 1994, the twenty-fifth anniversary of the Picasso reverse heist, we would recreate its return to honor my dad appropriately. I'd build a wooden crate to the same

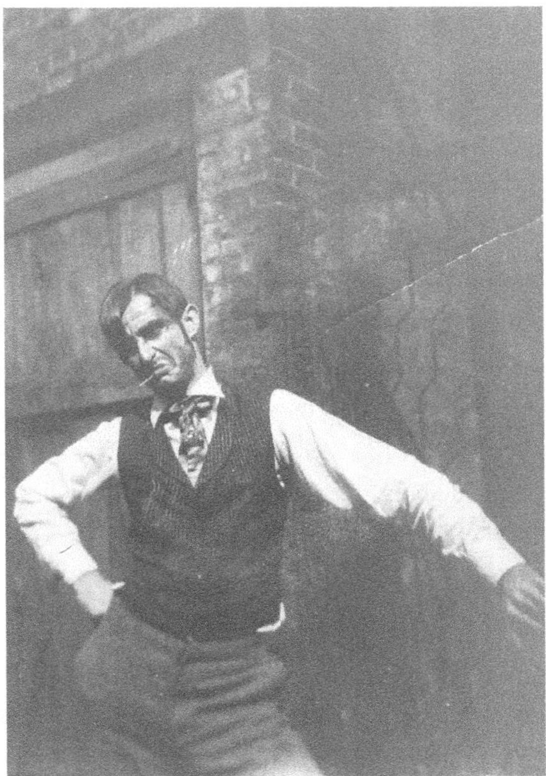

Figure 16.1 *Whit Sr., Equity Actor NYC, 1939*

specifications as the original crate that held the Picasso, then my brother and I would don disguises and drive the package to the same location in Boston. Next, we'd hail a cab, and one of us would give the crate to the unsuspecting cabbie and tell him just what to do. Then, we'd magically disappear. It would make all the papers, and we'd have a brand-new mystery we could celebrate!

It was perfect. I couldn't believe how clever I was to come up with something so ingenious. I immediately called Bill and told him about my wonderful plan for Robbin' Hood redux.

I must say, at this point in our relationship, we didn't communicate that frequently. His version of reality and mine were often at odds. But for something like this? How could he possibly say no?

It didn't take long. I started to explain the plan over the phone.

"You're nuts!"

That wasn't the enthusiasm I'd been after. He went on, "Why would you even *think* of doing something that crazy? We could get busted, for Chrissake! No way. Forget it."

And that was the end of that. I could have done it anyway, solo, but without his participation, it wouldn't have meant a thing.

My brother and I loved each other very much but didn't get along so well sometimes. That's probably obvious by now. We were inseparable until our teenage years, but grew up to be two very different people. The love never waned, but we didn't really seem to know what to do with one another, and so we were never close, aside from those moments linked to the Picasso affair.

For instance, my brother was seemingly unaffected by what I'd found in the chest, what I'd learned about our father. He barely reacted to it. I guess that Dad's early history wasn't really a puzzle to him, not a question that needed answering, anyway.

My mother was likewise nonplussed. By that time, she was eighty years old and not much moved her. Her reaction when I showed her all I'd found suggested that she didn't really understand what it was or the significance of it.

But now comes one of the many strange coincidences that befell during my never-ending Picasso adventure. The very next week after Bill's adamant "no," a good friend of mine, a fine actor named Will LeBow, called me. He happened to be part of ART, a well-known Cambridge theater group, and excitedly told me he'd been cast in a new play called *Picasso at the Lapin Agile*. It was a comedy about young Picasso and a meeting he'd had with Albert Einstein. It sounded fabulous, but the most exciting part of the call was that Will invited me to its preview premiere, and afterward, a dinner party with the playwright and the actors. The writer, who was wildly popular at the time, was Steve Martin. As in the world-famous comedian and actor, Steve Martin.

When the evening came, it was all I could have imagined. The play was great, funny, and intelligent. The dinner with Steve was amazing. During the meal, he and I had a great opportunity to talk one-on-one. I told him I'd always been a huge fan of Picasso. I went on to recount my experience of stealing a Picasso print from a library book when I was ten, and he found that amusing. He chuckled and said I'd go down in history as "Picasso's youngest art thief."

I could have continued my story and told him all about the Picasso reverse heist and how no one till that very moment had ever heard the story. And knowing Steve's penchant for wackiness, he might have grabbed it right there and run all the way with it. But I said nothing. It was my brother's story to tell, and I had no real right to it. At least back then, still fresh from Bill's insistence that the story remain buried, I didn't feel right in doing so. To this day, I wonder what would have happened had I told Steve the full story then. The vibe was right; we were seated next to each other at a long dinner, and amazingly enough, he was interested in me and my stories. It might have become a Hollywood film then and there.

For the next several years, nothing much happened with the Picasso story. Life went on, and I continued to have a great run with freelance producing. Good enough, at least, so I didn't have to worry about money.

Then came September 11, 2001. It was a very bad day, indeed, and it prompted me to give up corporate filmmaking. I'd had enough of that world, and it seemed banal when this sort of thing was happening in our backyard.

But what would I do instead? Corporate filmmaking and producing was all I'd done for the past twenty-five years. I gave it a lot of thought. What I decided on was reckless, maybe even a little stupid, but I needed to see if I could actually do it. I would go back to the old dream. I would write. More precisely, I would *screen* write.

Writing a script is a specialized craft. It's creating a blueprint for the movie, and it doesn't mean much beyond that—it's the movie that gets the kudos, while the script is just the plan from which the director and actors and hundreds of others build. I knew it was a long shot, but I gave myself two years to make something happen.

The idea for the script came to me on that horrific day of September 9, 2001, when I went to pick up my then twelve-year-old son from middle school. The story was about a young boy who kept the death of his older brother a secret, fearing that telling anyone would be too overwhelming. I called it *The Secret Boy*. The first draft took eight months. I did another draft and then another. Optimistic, I sent in an application, accompanied by the script, for a Nicholl Fellowship. It's awarded annually by the folks who bring you the Oscars: the

Academy of Motion Picture Arts and Sciences. I somehow managed to beat out 6,000 other entries and won one of the five fellowships. This included a week-long, all-expense-paid trip to Los Angeles and $30,000 in prize money—I even got an agent as well. To top everything off, the script was optioned for a sizable sum. I was on cloud nine.

In the meantime, Bill had retired and his stance on telling the Picasso story had softened. He no longer felt at risk. Decades had passed without his having been further investigated (as far as he was aware), much less imprisoned or "whacked."

He finally swayed into the "tell the story" lane when I received a contract to write an animated feature with one of our biggest childhood heroes, Walt Disney.

It turned out to be a heck of a lot of fun. It was called *Pigs Might Fly*. The folks at Disney loved it and were all set to move forward with it, but when a new studio head suddenly replaced the old, everything they'd championed was erased from the map, including my screenplay.

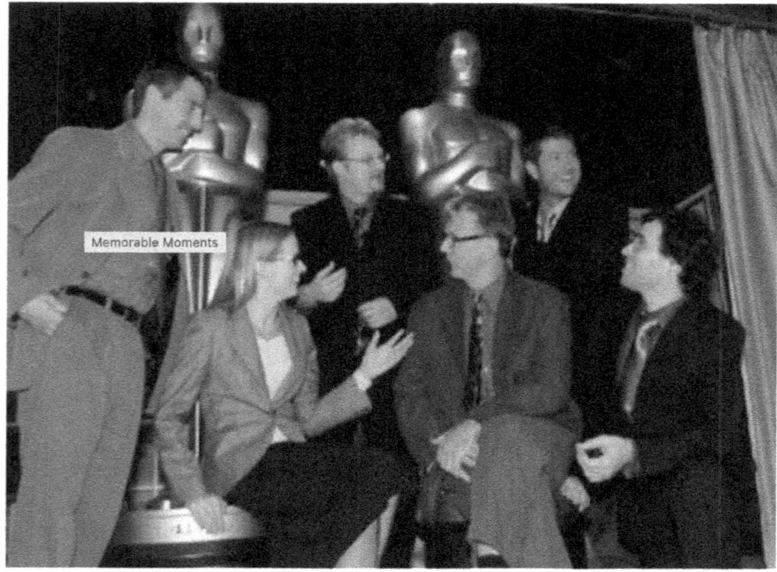

Figure 16.2 *Whit receiving The Academy's Nicholl Fellowship*

Regardless, Bill called to offer me carte blanche on the Picasso story. He told me I could write a feature in any way I saw fit. But he had one condition: "Just don't make me look too stupid." I laughed and assured him I wouldn't. I also guaranteed him 10 percent of whatever I made on the project. A good deal all around.

Ira Glass, the famed presenter and producer of National Public Radio's *This American Life,* which tells in-depth accounts of fascinating aspects of recent American history, had the same attorney as I did at the time. He heard about the reverse heist through her and contacted me about doing a story on it. Ira conducted an initial interview with Bill. Meanwhile, I began my own research on the project and made a call to Irving Luntz, the original buyer of the painting from Henry Kahnweiler in 1969.

Mr. Luntz was living in Palm Beach when I called him. He had moved from Milwaukee many years earlier. I asked him if he was the same Irving Luntz who had been the victim of a theft of a painting back in 1969. He let out a loud whoop and said, "I am!" Then he proceeded to tell me the story of that day with the famous Henry Kahnweiler and how exciting it was. He had a wonderful story to tell, and he related it to me in great detail. The following chapter is my own dramatization of those events, along with extensive research I'd done for the screenplay I was writing back then.

He remembered the entire event clearly. The following chapter is based on extensive research that informed my script as well as this book, laying out how Kahnweiler and Luntz made a deal for the Picasso in the first place.

17

Paris, France

January 1969

As Irving Luntz laid out to me over a long phone call, Paris on a cold winter day, January 9, 1969, to be precise, was slate gray.[1] This was Paris at its hippest, when everything cool on earth felt that it had been concentrated right there. It happened to be Luntz's fortieth birthday, and it would prove particularly fortuitous for him.

He felt clearly American, partly a byproduct of the way he was walking, briskly and with purpose through Parc Monceau, in a slick-looking suit and tweed overcoat.

Luntz had hardly slept the night before because today was going to be very special for this moderately successful gallery owner from Milwaukee (I added the "moderately successful" and a few other details to Luntz's story). He would meet someone he'd been reading about for many years, and he certainly didn't want to be late.

For Americans in the art world in the 1960s, there was a certain amount of European condescension to deal with. Since the Industrial Revolution, there'd been Americans with far more wealth and disposable income than what was available to European aristocrats, and the "robber barons" of the late nineteenth century had snapped up the best art that became available, often because the European aristocrats whose families had held it could no longer afford their swinging lifestyles and had to sell. This led to a power dynamic mixed with classism. The wealthy held the power, but wealthy Americans for the most part yearned for blue blood and couldn't buy it (with some exceptions, of course, the Rothschild family foremost among them). The European ancien régime was embarrassed that it had to sell off its treasures and did so with social reluctance but financial urgency.

When it came to modern, contemporary art, the dynamic was further compounded. The classiest of art dealers (or rather those that thought of themselves as such) dealt in the Old Masters, and for the most part disdained alternative contemporary movements of the twentieth century, like Cubism, Minimalism, and—heaven forbid because it was entirely American—Abstract Expressionism. Even the snooty snoots at the Metropolitan Museum of Art in New York, the high-brow museum of record in America, turned down donations of the best in twentieth-century art, considering it beneath them. It was only when some women collectors established their own museums—the Guggenheim, the Whitney, and the Museum of Modern Art—in Manhattan that twentieth-century art got its due, with the Metropolitan painfully slow to follow. So, if you liked art, and were American, that was one strike against you. If the art you liked was twentieth century rather than Old Master, that was two strikes. The Grand Central of Art in America was New York, so heaven help you if you wanted to be a player in the art world and you were based in, say . . . Milwaukee. And while the most prominent art historians and critics were Jewish, the same certainly didn't apply to dealers and gallerists, who could be both snooty and discriminatory.

Despite his sharp eye, Irving Luntz was an art world underdog. He'd been running Irving Gallery for a decade at that point and was doing quite well. He'd even been written up in local newspapers touting the importance of twentieth-century European art.

This trip to Paris was in hopes of making a significant acquisition. The only problem was that, while he'd been successful, he wasn't at the big-boy table when it came to cash in hand, so the most exciting pieces were usually outside of his budget. Still, he trusted his eye to find a reasonably priced purchase or two which he'd be able to flip for a reasonably high markup.

He turned onto Rue de Monceau, and his heart pinballed up to his throat as he approached number 47. He rang the doorbell with the understated brass plaque bearing the gallery's name.

The door buzzed, and Irving stepped inside.

Galerie Louise Leiris looked to be a perfect part of Paris' neoclassical nineteenth-century elegance from the outside, nestled among other gray stone edifices in the swanky 8th arrondissement. But once you entered, the traditional gave way to the contemporary. Many would have said back then that this was *the* gallery for modern painting. The walls were white, the frames clean, simple wood or metal, not one gilded or over-the-top. The works inside were a who's who of twentieth-century painting: Chagall, Miro, Picasso, Braque, Léger. Luntz had dealt in some of these names, but almost always in the form of prints, etchings, or lithographs. The walls were covered with *paintings* by these artists, most of which Luntz recognized instantly. He approached a secretary, who looked him up and down without hiding her evaluation.

"I believe Mr. Kahnweiler is expecting me? I'm Irving Luntz. From Milwaukee, in the United States." He handed her a business card.

"Mil ... wauk ... ee?" She sounded it out. It clearly wasn't ringing any bells. "Just a moment, sir, I'll let him know you are here."

While he waited, Luntz paced the main gallery space. One painting in particular, a fabulous Modigliani, caught his eye. A lovely baritone voice took him by surprise.

"Ah, Monsieur Luntz, of the Irving Gallery in Milwaukee, Wisconsin. What a pleasure to meet you."

Luntz turned around to find an elegant-looking elderly man. He was quite bald, with a prominent egg-shaped head, flanked by ears that stuck out to the side. He shook Luntz's hand heartily.

He was dressed immaculately in a three-piece suit, with a matching pocket square poofing out over his heart. His English was remarkably precise, though a slight European accent softened his words.

"It's an incredible honor to meet you, Monsieur Kahnweiler. I can't tell you how much I've been looking forward to this day." (Luntz remembered the dialogue this precisely, or else he invented it this precisely when he told it to me over the phone.)

Kahnweiler cocked his head sideways with a look of mock confusion. "Perhaps you've mistaken me for someone else," he replied.

"Oh no, I don't think so. I've been hoping to meet you for years. I've been following your career since I was a student."

Kahnweiler bowed modestly. "The honor is mine."

Luntz laughed. "Hardly, sir. And to honor this day, I arranged for it to happen on my birthday."

Kahnweiler did a double-take and grinned excitedly. "In that case, let me make a modest attempt to help you celebrate it!"

Henry Kahnweiler was so pivotal a figure in the history of modern art, best known for his role as a pioneering art dealer and advocate for Cubism, that he had been taught in Luntz's art history courses at the University of Chicago.

Born in 1884 in Mannheim, Germany, he grew up in a wealthy Jewish family with a strong cultural background. His early passion for art would lead him to Paris, the epicenter of the art world at the turn of the twentieth century, and until World War II, when New York took over that mantle.

In 1902, Kahnweiler moved to Paris, initially working as a stockbroker. But this was just to pay the bills and bide his time as he mingled with the vibrant art scene that was flourishing in the city. He frequented the cafés, like Closerie de Lilas, and studios, like Picasso's falling-apart squat called Bateau-Lavoir, where artists gathered. He immersed himself in the avant-garde movements of the time in the most organic way possible—by hanging out with the artists themselves.

By 1907, he had opened his own gallery, Galerie Kahnweiler, in the Rue Vignon. His vision was clear: to support and promote the most innovative artists of his generation, many of whom he called friends and few of whom were getting much attention from the establishment.

With a razor-sharp eye for talent, he quickly became a central figure in the promotion of Cubism, a revolutionary artistic movement that sought to break away from traditional perspectives and represent objects from multiple angles simultaneously. Luntz had imagined Cubism as a photograph of a subject that has been cut into irregular pieces, shuffled around, and pasted back together haphazardly. You can sort of tell what the subject is, but the point is to shatter perspective and shift organic lines into geometry.

Kahnweiler was one of the first to recognize the genius of Pablo Picasso, Georges Braque, and Juan Gris, among others. He not only provided them with financial support by purchasing their works but also offered them creative freedom and stability by establishing long-term contracts.

His belief in Cubism was not just a business strategy but a genuine intellectual engagement with the movement. Kahnweiler was deeply influenced by the ideas of the French philosopher Henri Bergson, whose concepts of time and perception resonated with the Cubist approach to breaking down and reassembling visual reality. Kahnweiler became a passionate advocate for the movement, publishing essays and organizing exhibitions that introduced Cubism to a wider audience.

Some would say that, without Kahnweiler, those great artists, Picasso foremost among them as the most celebrated artist of the twentieth century and the most recognized artistic name of all time, might have languished, either longer or indefinitely, in obscurity.

But Kahnweiler's career was dramatically disrupted by the outbreak of World War I in 1914. As a German national, he was declared an enemy alien by the French government, and his gallery's assets, including hundreds of artworks, were confiscated and auctioned off. This was a devastating blow, but Kahnweiler was determined to rebuild.

After the war, Kahnweiler reestablished himself under the name Galerie Simon, distancing his business from the wartime stigma associated with his German origins and surname. He continued to champion modern art, now with a focus on maintaining the legacy of Cubism while also supporting new talents. His ability to recover from the loss and continue his work is a testament to his resilience and dedication to the artists he believed in.

Luntz admired not only Kahnweiler's eye and resilience but also his ability to thrive in an environment marked by various levels of antisemitism, from subtle to overt and violent.

In the 1920s and 1930s, Kahnweiler's gallery remained a crucial venue for modern art, helping to shape the tastes of collectors and the direction of contemporary art. He was also instrumental in publishing key texts on Cubism, which helped to solidify its place in art history. This had been assigned reading when Luntz was a student in Chicago.

The outbreak of World War II again posed significant challenges for Kahnweiler, who, being Jewish, faced persecution under the Vichy regime. He went into hiding, and his gallery was managed by his associate and stepdaughter, Louise Leiris. After the war, the gallery was renamed Galerie Louise Leiris. This was not only a way to evade anti-German and anti-Jewish sentiment but it also passed the torch to Leiris as one of Paris' leading art influencers, so that her career and the gallery continued to thrive when Kahnweiler passed away ten years later, at age ninety-four. The only trouble was that he was so long-lived that she only lived another two years before she too passed away.

But on that day in early 1969, Kahnweiler was a sprightly 84-year-old, and he'd invited Irving to a nearby patisserie for a treat.

A small, half-eaten, single-portion birthday cake sat between the two men as they sipped their cafés au lait.

"I first met the young Picasso through our mutual acquaintances in the Paris art scene. I took no time at all to offer him a contract. I could see from the very first he was a shining star and wanted to represent him before he got too big for a young man like me. At the time, I had a lovely moustache and lots of dark hair, if you can imagine. The year was 1907, the same year he broke out with his first celebrated work, *Les Demoiselles d'Avignon*," Kahnweiler recounted.

Luntz nodded excitedly. "Not long ago, I read a *Life* magazine interview with him in which he joked about having stolen statue heads from the Louvre that very same year. Incredibly, they appeared as the faces of the ladies in that painting. He thought of it all as a big joke, but that's quite special, isn't it? To have stolen from the Louvre and gotten away with it?"

"Ah yes, they call it the *affaire des statuettes*," Kahnweiler recalled. "I'm not sure if 'special' is the right word, but it's certainly the word for Picasso. Pity you can't meet him while you're here; he's at his maison in the south and rarely comes to Paris these days."

Luntz couldn't believe what he was hearing. Even imagining that he would be able to meet Picasso sounded marvelous. In his wildest dreams, he'd never thought he would be where he was with a man who could actually make that happen.

Kahnweiler set his cup down and leaned in closer to Irving. "So, my friend, am I right in assuming you're looking to acquire some pieces for your gallery while you're here in Paris?"

Luntz nodded. "But my funds are certainly limited. I'm not sure I'd be able to afford anything from the famous *Galerie Louise Leiris*, Monsieur Kahnweiler."

"Please, call me Henry. And I'll call you Irving, if I may. It will be so much nicer like that." Luntz emphasized this part in his retelling—he loved it. Kahnweiler stood and set a handful of francs on the table.

"Why don't you let me show you some things, now that we know one another." He paused, then gave Luntz a mysterious wink. "Perhaps even some *special* things."

At the gallery, they walked past the woman at the desk, past all the paintings and sculptures in the main display area, and into the back of the shop.

Finally, they came to a wrought-iron spiral staircase leading to a cellar below.

"Follow me," Kahnweiler said, as they descended the steps.

In a large space below, Kahnweiler turned on the lights that instantly illuminated the entire area. Rows of sliding stacks along one wall contained hundreds of reference books. Further along, cabinets and shelving held important, smaller sculpture pieces. There were exquisite color photo reproductions of famous works on display that the gallery had sold over the years.

They passed through a security gate that Kahnweiler unlocked with a special key and entered a large, climate-controlled room. An ornate lighting scheme automatically kicked on.

Luntz gasped. The room was filled with magnificent pieces that he immediately recognized, exceeding even what he'd seen upstairs. Works he actually knew by name and date straight away, having studied them, or longed for them, or both.

"My special collection. Mostly not for sale," Kahnweiler said. "I keep them here because it's safer than my apartment. Over sixty years of history here. Some purchased, but most gifts from the artists. They represent a lifetime of friendships."

"I feel like I'm standing in the midst of Heaven," Luntz said, in awe.

Kahnweiler chuckled, "Come now, my friend. People like us don't believe in Heaven, do we?" He turned serious. "But I know what you mean. I feel the same way in their presence."

Luntz noticed that at least ten of the works were actually portraits of Kahnweiler himself. By Juan Gris, Kees van Dongen, and others, including Picasso (one in pencil featured a humorously exaggerated egghead and over-large ears).

There was also a giant reclining nude, very Cubist and very Picasso, taller and wider than a grown man, which covered most of one wall. Kahnweiler nodded toward the nude.

"That's supposed to be me, believe it or not," he said. "Though I don't see much resemblance myself. I used to keep it behind my desk in my upstairs office, to impress the dignitaries."

Kahnweiler noticed that Luntz was not looking at the nude anymore; something else had drawn his eye—another painting, also by Picasso, but considerably smaller.

"That's quite something, is it not?" Kahnweiler said. "A gift. During one of my recent visits to Notre-Dame-de-Vie in Mougins near Cannes. The oil is barely dry."

"It's absolutely breathtaking," Luntz whispered, as much to himself as to his host.

"Do you know about the subject?"

"A bit," Luntz admitted. "But I'd like nothing more than for you to tell me more."

Kahnweiler laughed. "Very well. Picasso first began painting the subject of the musketeer around 1966. He's been interested in revisiting and reinterpreting historical figures, particularly those from the seventeenth century, such as musketeers. You're probably familiar with *Les Trois Musketeers*. Someday they should make a film out of it. It would be a good one. Suddenly, he's painting and drawing and etching these musketeers, among his plentiful menagerie of themes, including minotaurs and such. He especially likes to pair them with female figures, as you can see. Sex, love, power, basically the interplay between masculine and feminine energies. And muskets standing in for, well, you can imagine."

"I certainly can," Luntz giggled. He couldn't believe that he was being told about Picasso by the man who actually made Picasso's career, there in a very private room in a very exclusive gallery.

"Scholars will tell you that the pairing of the woman and the musketeer in Picasso's work symbolizes a dialogue between different archetypes—often exploring the dynamic between the assertive, adventurous spirit of the musketeer and the serene, often idealized image of the Woman. I think it's simply about penises more than anything else, but then, I'm not a scholar." Kahnweiler winked. "I think he painted the first work of this subject in 1966. This one was done two years ago."

"It's truly stunning."

"Tell me, Irving. Would you like to buy it?"

Luntz did a noticeable double-take. "Of course . . . I mean, *most certainly I would*. But—I could never afford it, not at the moment, anyway. Perhaps, in a year or two . . .

Kahnweiler mused for a moment. "How old are you today, my friend? If it's not too forward a question."

"I'm forty," Luntz answered.

Kahnweiler thought for a moment. "Forty. I like to think that it's not quite midlife—if it were, I'd have been buried years ago—but it's exactly the time when the greatest things happen to those in our line of work."

He walked over to the painting and studied it carefully. Then he turned back to Luntz.

"Shall we say forty, then?"

Luntz could hardly catch his breath. "Forty? But I don't understand, it must be worth five times that!"

Kahnweiler smiled modestly. "At least."

"Why would you . . . ?" Luntz sought the words.

Kahnweiler patted him on the shoulder lightly. "Who can really put a reasonable price on anything in this life, my friend? The relativity of value is a mysterious and elusive thing. Much like love, I suppose."

Luntz still couldn't register what Kahnweiler was telling him.

"Listen," Kahnweiler continued. "When you reach an age as ripe as mine, you come to realize that it's not so much about maximizing the income, but about how people will remember you when you're no longer there to remind them. I got the painting for free—as a gift—so don't worry about me. I'm still making a very reasonable profit. Just consider it a birthday gift and my hope that your gallery becomes an even bigger success."

Luntz shook his head in disbelief. "I . . . I don't know what to say."

"A simple thank-you will do perfectly well."

Later, the two men stood in front of the secretary as she handed Irving Luntz some papers. "I'll arrange the carnet and have it boxed and shipped by air to your gallery in Milwaukee."

Luntz nearly teared up. "Thank you so much, Henry. I'll never forget this day. It's the best gift I've ever received."

"Not a gift, Irving, simply an incentive. To do more business with me in the future. I hope to see you back here often."

Luntz laughed. "Of that, you can be absolutely certain, *mon ami!*"

They gave each other a warm embrace at the entrance. Then Luntz exited, a spring in his step. The painting would ship from Paris to Milwaukee, via Boston. It would be his shortly. Everything was going according to plan.

18

2007–2009

In 2007, Mr. Luntz was living in Palm Beach, having moved from Milwaukee many years earlier. When I finally called him, I asked him if he was the same Irving Luntz who had been the victim of a theft in transit of a painting back in 1969; he let out a loud whoop and said, "I am!" Then he proceeded to tell me the story of that day with the famous Henry Kahnweiler, and how exciting it was. This conversation was the basis for the previous chapter.

He went on to tell me how shocked and depressed he'd been after learning of the painting's theft. But then, when he told me about the painting's return by the mysterious "Robbin' Hood," he let out another whoop and declared, "I could've reached right across the country and given that Robbin' Hood a great big hug!"

It was a thrilling call, and when I got home, I started to tell my wife about it. "But what did he say when you told him *your* side of the story?" she asked excitedly. "I didn't," I said. "What?" she cried. I shrugged. "Because it's Bill's story to tell, and I have to wait for him to do it."

Around that time, I also made a call to Ed Corsetti, the well-known *Boston Herald* reporter who had penned several articles about the missing Picasso in 1969. He had retired by then, in his late seventies, and he remembered the story well. When I asked him (without revealing my role in the affair) if they'd ever caught the thief, he replied, "No, they didn't." But then he commented that they were almost certain it was Whitey Bulger who had been behind it all, because he'd also been involved in the world-famous Isabella Stewart Gardner heist in 1990, which remains unsolved.

When I hung up, I was floored. In all of my research about the details of the theft, that was the first time I'd ever heard Whitey's name attached as someone suspected of involvement, some forty years after it had gone down. I thought it was amusing. How could they be so far off from what had really happened?

I phoned Bill and told him about my call to Corsetti, and how crazy that was. But Bill didn't think it was funny at all. On the contrary, he was alarmed. At that time, in 2007, Whitey was still on the lam and was definitely considered an active threat to any and all who had crossed him. The FBI had been searching for him since 1995, so at that point, twelve years. He wouldn't be caught until 2011. If Whitey even *thought* that Bill might have had something to do with it, who knew what could happen? Logically speaking, Whitey wasn't going to come out of hiding to take revenge on a stranger who had accidentally swiped a painting forty years before that Whitey might have theoretically wanted to swipe, but Bill wasn't thinking logically. Once again, my attempt to foresee Bill's delighted reaction proved off-target. No, he hadn't wanted to recreate the crime as a prank in honor of our deceased father, and no, he didn't think it was funny at all that Whitey Bulger was thought to have been involved in *his* theft. Bill then told me he didn't want anything to do with the project—that was the end of the film version of our Picasso story.

I had no choice but to abide by his wishes. After all, maybe Whitey really *was* a danger? The screenplay was set aside.

It was 2009, and I became depressed. I'd just turned sixty-three. The only real money I'd made since I began screenwriting was the Disney gig, and it was evaporating swiftly. I wasn't getting any younger, either. I began to think that any chance I had of making *it* had ended.

I got this crazy notion to thru-hike the Appalachian Trail. Not my first crazy notion, nor the last. It was something that would undoubtedly turn my life upside-down, but I needed something drastic to make that happen. I needed a reset. I needed to shake myself out of my torpor. To get up off the couch.

Having grown up in the wilds of Maine, you might think that I was a rugged and bearded, knife-carrying, bear-wrestling hiker. Truth is, I'd never even been on an overnight hike before and knew absolutely nothing about camping. But suddenly it was something I just had to do.

So, with frighteningly little preparation, I was dropped off at the base of Springer Mountain in Georgia on March 5 and started my solo trek. Everyone had advised that it was much too early in the year to start, but that day was important to me, perhaps the most important day of my life, because it was the day I turned the same age my father had been on the day he died. I'd always been afraid of it. After all, I was used to everybody saying that I was just like him: the same fingers and toes (though not exactly the ones that I was born with), the same sense of humor; I even had the exact same name he had. Why should I think I'd outlast him?

The first day was endless. And very cold. The next day was the same. So was the third. And the fourth. But I kept walking. Along the way, my father and I had some wonderful conversations about things we never said to each other when he was alive. Long periods of solo trekking will do that to you.

Four and a half months later, forty-five pounds lighter, and after 2,181 miles, I ended up climbing Mount Katahdin in northern Maine, the official end of the trail. It was the hardest thing I'd ever done.

I was a new man.

I came back with a renewed sense of optimism and energy and immediately jumped back into the Picasso script. I decided to write a fictionalized version, and as a matter of fact, Whitey Bulger became a major character in the script; a part of it even included his direct involvement in the Gardner Museum heist. Personally, I thought it was pretty damn good. And in June of 2011, I decided to take it to Los Angeles and pitch it to some producers I knew.

I spent the week going around to several production houses, introducing the heist script. The interest was mostly around Whitey's part. After all, he was America's Most Wanted criminal. The day before I was to leave, a friend and I were sitting on the Third Street Promenade in Santa Monica, sipping lattes and discussing my recent pitch-fest, when people started running past us on the street.

"They got him!" they were saying.

"Got who?" we asked.

"Whitey!" they yelled.

"Really? Are you kidding me?"

We jumped up and followed. No one is going to believe this coincidence, I thought, if it really is what I think it is.

Less than two blocks away, the apartment where Whitey Bulger and his paramour had been living for several years was under siege. Police cars surrounded it, yellow tape blocked it off, reporters milled around, a crowd gawked. Whitey and his girlfriend had been hauled away in cuffs shortly before our arrival, but it was still chaos. He'd been on the run, in hiding, for sixteen years. And yet he'd been living for much of it in a nice part of Los Angeles, chatting with neighbors, walking his dog, literally hiding in plain sight.[1]

A Boston reporter grabbed me and asked what I was doing there. He ran video as I breathlessly told him, ever so briefly, about the stolen Picasso and Whitey. How could it possibly be just a coincidence? It was just too much, one in a million. See this video and more at stealingpicasso.com.

Within minutes, I called Bill, who by this time was living in Charleston, South Carolina. I told him what had happened. He couldn't believe it either.

But then, he said, "I guess it's about time we get our story out there, don't you?"

You bet I did.

The fictionalized screenplay instantly went out the window because Whitey's whereabouts were no longer a mystery. The true story could now be a true story again. At last, we could tell the *real* story!

I went back home full of new and exciting ideas. One of the first things I did was call Irving Luntz again to set up an interview with him and my brother.

Once more, without revealing my end of the story, I asked him if he'd be willing to be interviewed. He seemed intrigued by it all and said yes. I contacted Bill, and he agreed to drive down to Palm Beach with me for the event. During the interview between Mr. Luntz and Bill, my brother would reveal his role in the whole thing. Surprise! Mr. Luntz would be gobsmacked. I'd get it all on camera.

The interview was set, but then my brother's health worsened. He'd been diagnosed with lung cancer a couple of years earlier, and his situation grew grim. He'd had a serious flare-up and couldn't make it to the interview. When Bill was asked why he didn't quit smoking, he'd reply, "Well, you know what Dad would say."

"What?" folks would reply.

"Nobody likes a quitter."

It was a little dance that we did together more than once. His idea of humor.

We rescheduled. His health didn't improve. We kept postponing. The interview never happened.

Bill passed away in May of 2015.

Grief has a way of taking the fun out of things. I was devastated. The only person who could really vouch for me ever *being* a kid in the first place was gone. The idea of making a fun movie about the single most exciting event in our lives vanished. The Picasso story seemed to die with him.

That might have been the end of it all.

19

2019

Stubborn old me, I still wouldn't call it quits. Not without getting this wonderful story out to the public somehow. In 2019, the fiftieth anniversary of our perfect crime, I decided to give it one last try. I wrote up a short history of the whole thing and sent it to a number of newspapers, hoping someone might be interested. In almost no time, Richard Just, at the time the editor of *The Washington Post Sunday Magazine*, sent me a note telling me he was very intrigued. The only problem, he said, was not knowing what had happened to the painting. Apparently, it dropped off the face of the earth soon after its return in 1969. We tried to find any record. Nothing. And without proof the painting had ever existed, the story was a bust. At least, from his perspective. Just because something is lost doesn't make a story involving it any less intriguing. But the *Post* passed on it.

Again, I was heartbroken, but I couldn't give it up. The only mention of the painting's current whereabouts after its return was during one of the conversations I had with Irving Luntz. He mentioned selling it soon after it was returned by Robbin' Hood.

When I'd pressed him, he'd been, quite naturally, evasive and wouldn't tell me who'd bought it. But he did say that, as far as he knew, the original buyers were still in possession of it. I would have loved to phone Irving one last time to get more details. Alas, he passed away in 2018 at the age of eighty-eight, without ever having heard the real story of how his Picasso got "delayed" en route from Paris to Milwaukee in the winter of 1969.

I had another idea. I'd been looking for information on the painting for decades, but that didn't mean that I was any kind of expert. I decided to ask a friend, well-known journalist Will Blythe, if he knew of a "cyber-sleuth," someone who might be able to track it down on the internet, because I had given up all hope. In an instant, he had an idea.

"Monica Boyer. If anyone could track it down, she can."

I called her ten minutes later. She listened to my tale, then said she'd give it a try. No promises, of course, but worth a try.

Three days later, I got a call. Monica had found something: a catalog from 1971 titled "Picasso in Milwaukee," from the Milwaukee Arts Center (now The Milwaukee Art Museum). Inside were various works of art loaned to the art center for an exhibit of Picasso's work, all of them owned by local private patrons. Lo and behold, on page 22 was an image of *Portrait of a Woman and a Musketeer*, identical to our long-lost portrait. The full entry is:

> *Portrait of a Woman and a Musketeer*
> 21–30 March 1967
> Oil on canvas, 39 3/8 x 31 7/8
> Mr. and Mrs. Sidney Kohl[1]

It was work number 11 in the catalog, the exhibition running from October 25 to November 28.

Finally, after fifty years, I was staring at irrefutable evidence that it actually exists. Just as surprising were the owners attributed to the work: Sidney and Dorothy Kohl. I immediately looked them up.

The Kohls, now well into their nineties, had long ago moved to Palm Beach. Sidney Kohl was a scion of the Kohl's department store empire and was still active in art collecting. In 2012, for example, part of his Abstract Expressionist collection had sold for 101 million dollars. Wow.

I tried for months to contact them: first through e-mail, then by phone, and finally, through a hand-written letter. Nothing. As a last resort, I tried an old LAN line I discovered on the internet. I called.

After a ring or two, someone answered.

It was Dorothy Kohl. She was surprised to hear what I was calling about: a Picasso painting of a lady and a musketeer that they'd bought way back when.

She didn't deny that they still had it and told me to speak to Sidney for more information. He'd gone shopping but would be back in an hour. I thanked her and hung up.

The next hour seemed like an eternity.

I finally called back. Dorothy answered again, then handed the phone to Sidney. I immediately launched into my story but was abruptly interrupted. "Don't you ever call this number again," Sidney said.

Then he hung up.

Finally, I knew *exactly* where the painting had been all these years.

But I wasn't finished. In early 2023, I contacted Jesse Drucker, a senior financial writer for the *New York Times*, telling him my story. Drucker handed my letter to someone else at the *Times*, Kevin Flynn, the features editor. Flynn found it intriguing enough to assign it to Dan Barry, a Pulitzer Prize-winning journalist.

Bingo. It had landed in the exact right spot.

On Father's Day of 2023, an article appeared on the front page of the *New York Times* with the title, "Hey Dad, Can You Help Me Return the Picasso I Stole?" It was perfectly delightful and reprinted in dozens of papers around the world. A viral success.

Another event happened that Father's Day as well. My son Whit, who is thirty-five as I write, was home for the weekend when he presented me with an amazingly accurate forgery of the original painting. He happens to be an excellent artist, along with many other skills, and it looks very much like it could be the original. Picasso is the most-forged artist of the modern era, after all. It's difficult to say for sure, because the original painting has never, to my knowledge, been photographed in color, but my son sought out other Picasso paintings from the late 1960s to get an idea of the color palette that Picasso was using then. What a gift. We were unable to reproduce the work here, but see it and more at stealingpicasso.com.

A few weeks later, Swiss public television contacted me about doing a story on the subject. I was happy to oblige. Producer Massimiliano Berger and his cameraman came to Chapel Hill and spent a day filming. Only a few days later, a wonderful televised story about the theft came out.

My dream had finally come true.

Almost.

Right after the theft, I thought that surely the painting would appear in some museum. Surely Luntz would loan it out for an exhibit? The plan was that, as soon as that happened, the three of us—Bill, Dad, and I—would have our picture taken in front of it, smiling innocently. No one would know. Except us. It would be the ultimate souvenir, the ultimate inside joke.

Years after my father's passing, I imagined Bill and me having our picture taken with it, standing in that same museum and smiling secretly, nobody knowing but us.

Now, I have a vision that one day, I'll have *my* picture taken in front of it. But it won't just be me; it'll feature the three remaining Whits: me, my son, and my nephew, all named after the same wonderful man. And we'll be smiling, proudly and loudly now, because our story has finally been told.

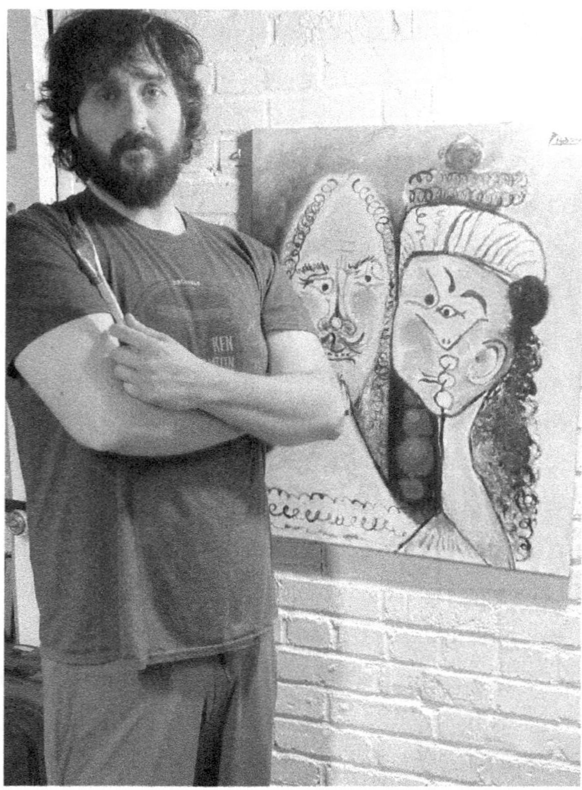

Figure 19.1 *A painting done in 2023 by Whitcomb Cambell Rummel. The painting is fake but pays homage to the Picasso work stolen by the Rummel family in 1969.*

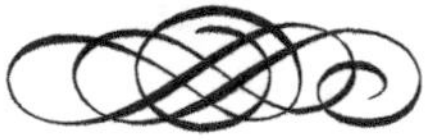

Notes

Introduction

1   Dan Barry, "Hey Dad, Can You Help Me Return the Picasso I Stole?" *The New York Times*, June 15, 2023, viewable at https://www.nytimes.com/2023/06/15/arts/design/stolen-picasso-boston.html.

Chapter 2

1   Frank Sleeper, "A Little Extra Effort Pays Off," *The Waterville Morning Sentinel*, October 2, 1968.

2   "It's Round, Black and Made to Sell Ice Cream," *Waterville Daily Sentinel*, July 28, 1951.

Chapter 3

1   "Rummel's Maine Mile Contest," *Waterville Morning Sentinel*, August 21, 1967.

Chapter 4

1   Quote from an original menu from the restaurant preserved in the author's archive.

2   These quotes were posted on a Facebook group at the address https://www.facebook.com/groups/6189527620/ that was active in November 2024 but appears to no longer be active.

3   Susan Sterling, "The Last Page: Her Head on Straight," *Colby Magazine* 91, no. 3 (2002): article 10.

4   Referenced in Sterling, "The Last Page," *Colby Magazine*, 2002.

Chapter 5

1 Frank Sleeper, "A Little Extra Effort Pays Off." *The Waterville Morning Sentinel*, October 2, 1968.

2 Ibid.

Chapter 7

1 The interview with National Public Radio was transcribed and is part of the author's archive, but the interview was never published.

Chapter 8

1 "Fire, Flames Damage Rummel's Ice Cream Plant, Store," *Waterville Morning Sentinel*, February 21, 1969.

2 "Fire, Flames Damage Rummel's Ice Cream Plant, Store," *Waterville Morning Sentinel*, February 21, 1969.

3 This is the aforementioned transcript, which is in the author's archive but was never published.

Chapter 12

1 "Robbin Hood Ends Lost Picasso Puzzle," *The Boston Globe*, March 29, 1969.

2 Ed Corsetti and Maureen Taylor, "Case of the Stolen Picassos-International Gang in Hub?" *The Boston Globe*, March 30, 1969.

3 Corsetti and Taylor, "Case of the Stolen Picassos," *The Boston Globe*, 1969.

4 Noah Charney, *Museum of Lost Art* (New York: Phaidon, 2018), 30.

5 Sanka Knox, "Museum Gets Rembrandt for 2.3 Million," *The New York Times*, November 16, 1961.

6 Bulger's life story is told in many places, but the most comprehensive is D. Lehr and G. O'Neill, *Whitey: The Life of America's Most Notorious Mob Boss* (New York: Crown, 2013).

Chapter 17

1   This account comes from a personal call between the author and Luntz.

Chapter 18

1   "Fugitive Mobster Whitey Bulger Busted in Santa Monica," *Santa Monica Daily*, June 23, 2011, https://smdp.com/news/fugitive-mobster-whitey-bulger-busted-in-santa-monica/.

Chapter 19

1   The catalog is in the author's archive.

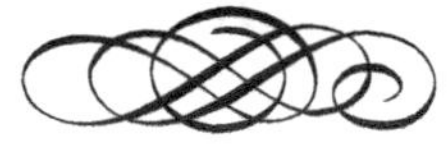

Bibliography and Further Reading

This is not a traditionally researched book, but primarily my personal retelling, the insider's story, of a quirky and renowned American art theft. Almost all of it comes from my own memory supplemented by some newspaper articles from which quotes were drawn. There has been no book about this incident in particular until now. The bibliography consists mostly of articles cited (note that not all articles had author bylines when published, which is why the author is not listed). I've also included suggestions for further reading on art theft and Picasso.

Selected Bibliography

Barry, Dan. "Hey Dad, Can You Help Me Return the Picasso I Stole?" *The New York Times*, June 15, 2023.

Charney, Noah. *Museum of Lost Art*. Phaidon, 2018.

Charney, Noah. *The Thefts of the Mona Lisa*. Lanham, MD: Rowman & Littlefield, 2023.

Corsetti, Ed., and Maureen Taylor. "Case of the Stolen Picassos-International Gang in Hub?" *The Boston Globe*, March 30, 1969.

Knox, Sanka. "Museum Gets Rembrandt for 2.3 Million." *The New York Times*, November 16, 1961.

Lehr, D., and G. O'Neill. *Whitey: The Life of America's Most Notorious Mob Boss*. New York: Crown, 2013.

Sleeper, Frank. "A Little Extra Effort Pays Off." *The Waterville Morning Sentinel*, October 2, 1968.

Sterling, Susan. "The Last Page: Her Head on Straight." *Colby Magazine* 91, no. 3 (2002): article 10.

Further Reading

Assouline, Pierre. *An Artful Life: A Biography of D. H. Kahnweiler 1884–1979*. New York: Fromm International, 1991.

FitzGerald, Michael C. *Making Modernism: Picasso and the Creation of the Market for Twentieth-Century Art*. New York: Farrar, Straus and Giroux, 1995.

Gilot, Françoise, and Carlton Lake. *Life with Picasso*. New York: McGraw-Hill, 1964.

Parkinson, Gavin. *Picasso: The Lost Sketchbook*. London: Pallas Athene, 2024.

Richardson, John. *A Life of Picasso: The Prodigy, 1881–1906*. New York: Random House, 1991.

Richardson, John. *A Life of Picasso: The Cubist Rebel, 1907–1916*. New York: Alfred A. Knopf, 1996.

Richardson, John. *A Life of Picasso: The Minotaur Years, 1933–1943*. New York: Alfred A. Knopf, 2010.

Richardson, John. *A Life of Picasso: The Triumphant Years, 1917–1932*. New York: Alfred A. Knopf, 2007.

Warncke, Carsten-Peter. *Pablo Picasso: 1881–1973*. Cologne: Taschen, 1998.

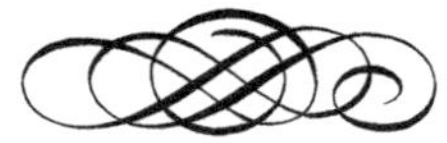

Index

Note: The following is a selected index with certain keywords, like "Picasso," excluded since they appear so often.

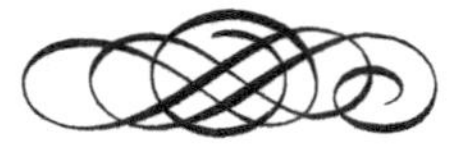

About the Authors

Whit Rummel Jr. is an award-winning screenwriter and filmmaker. He has spent his professional lifetime working in almost every aspect of filmmaking. After graduating with a Master's in Film from Boston University, he began his career as a documentarian. His first project, *TATTOO*, was a quirky 16mm film about heavily tattooed people that aired nationally on the PBS series, *Independent Focus*.

He went on to establish WITCOM Associates, a Boston-based production house specializing in innovative programming for corporate and commercial clients. With an excellent staff of producers and Whit directing, the company quickly grew into one of New England's premier production houses, working with dozens of Fortune 500 companies, including IBM, Microsoft, GM, RJR Nabisco, DuPont, Motorola, Sony, Exxon, and Citicorp.

After many years immersed in the corporate world, Whit sold WITCOM to a national communications company in order to spend time on his own personal passions. His first screenplay, *Secret Boy*, was awarded the Nicholl Fellowship from the Academy of Motion Picture Arts and Sciences. He was contracted by DisneyToon Studios to script an animated feature called *Pigs Might Fly*. A number of his other spec scripts have also been optioned.

Besides a Master's in Film, Whit holds a BA in Sociology from Tulane University. He served in the United States Marine Corps.

Dr. Noah Charney is the internationally best-selling author of more than twenty-nine books, translated into fourteen languages, including *The Collector of Lives: Giorgio Vasari and the Invention of Art*, which was nominated for the 2017 Pulitzer Prize in Biography, and *Museum of Lost Art,* which was a finalist for the 2018 Digital Book World Award. He is a professor of art history specializing in art crime and has taught for Yale University, Brown University, American University of Rome, and University of Ljubljana. He is the founder of ARCA, the Association for Research into Crimes against Art, a groundbreaking research group (www.artcrimeresearch.org) and teaches on their annual summer-long Postgraduate Program in Art Crime and Cultural Heritage Protection. He has written for dozens of major magazines and newspapers, including *The Guardian, The Washington Post, The Observer,* and *The Art Newspaper.* His recent books on art include *The Devil in the Gallery: How Scandal, Shock and Rivalry Shaped the Art World; Making It: The Artist's Survival Guide; The 12-Hour Art Expert: Everything You Need to Know About Art in a Dozen Masterpieces;* and *Brushed Aside: The Untold Story of Women in Art,* several of which were Amazon #1 bestsellers in their category. He also published the critically acclaimed *The Slavic Myths* in the fall of 2023 and *The Thefts of the Mona Lisa: The Complete Story of the World's Most Famous Artwork* (February 2024), which was praised in the *New York Times Book Review* and the *Telegraph,* among others. He fronted an influencer campaign for Samsung. In 2022, he presented a BBC Radio 4 documentary, *China's Stolen Treasures;* his TED Ed videos (some on art crime) have been viewed by millions each; and he featured in a recent Amazon Prime documentary, *The Picasso of Thieves.* He teaches for The Teaching Company's Great Courses and online for the National Gallery (UK), the Smithsonian, and Yale University. He lives in Slovenia with his wife, children, and their hairless dog, Hubert van Eyck (believe it or not). For more info, images, videos and material on this story, please visit the official website for this book, stealingpicasso.com.